The ESS of

AUDITING

Frank C. Giove, M.B.A., CPA
Associate Professor of Accounting
Niagara University, New York

 Research and Education Association
61 Ethel Road West
Piscataway, New Jersey 08854

THE ESSENTIALS® OF AUDITING

Printed in the United States of America

Library of Congress Catalog Card Number 92-81014

International Standard Book Number 0-87891-879-5

ESSENTIALS is a registered trademark of
Research & Education Association, Piscataway, New Jersey 08854

WHAT "THE ESSENTIALS" WILL DO FOR YOU

This book is a review and study guide. It is comprehensive and it is concise.

It helps in preparing for exams, in doing homework, and remains a handy reference source at all times.

It condenses the vast amount of detail characteristic of the subject matter and summarizes the **essentials** of the field.

It will thus save hours of study and preparation time.

The book provides quick access to the important facts, principles, theorems, concepts, and functions in the field.

Materials needed for exams can be reviewed in summary form – eliminating the need to read and re-read many pages of textbook and class notes. The summaries will even tend to bring detail to mind that had been previously read or noted.

This "ESSENTIALS" book has been prepared by an expert in the field, and has been carefully reviewed to assure accuracy and maximum usefulness.

Dr. Max Fogiel
Program Director

CONTENTS

3   Professional Ethics

4   Legal Liability 24

5   Engagement Planning 32

6 Internal Control Structure in Manually Operated Systems 39

9 Audit Techniques 64

14 Other Types of Engagements and Reports 108

CHAPTER 1

AUDIT FUNCTION

1.1 Definition of Auditing

Auditing is the process of examining the assertions or representations of another party and providing assurance on the fairness and reliability of the information in accordance with given standards.

When applied to accounting, auditing means having an independent auditor (defined later) attest to the fairness of the financial statements of an entity in conformity to generally accepted accounting principles (GAAP). GAAP represent the conventions, rules, and standards that govern the reporting of accounting information in the financial statements.

This book deals with auditing in relation to financial statements, that is the work of independent or external auditors as opposed to internal auditors.

1.2 Types of Audits

There are two basic types of audits:

1. *Compliance audits* attest to the fairness of the information versus given standards, e.g., financial statements in conformity with GAAP.

2. *Operational audits* measure the efficiency and effectiveness of a particular operation or unit or department of a business.

1.3 External and Internal Auditors

Users of financial statements strongly desire an objective opinion on the fairness of the financial statements. Thus, independent or external auditors lend credibility to the assertions or representations made by management via the financial statements.

External or outside auditors audit financial statements and may perform other attest functions or even operational audits when engaged by clients. In contrast, auditors on the payroll of companies or internal auditors carry out operational audits and do not and cannot perform financial statement compliance audits. Only external auditors qualified as CPAs or Certified Public Accountants can attest to the fairness of an entity's financial statements. To qualify as a CPA, a person must meet certain educational and experience requirements as well as pass a rigorous examination on accounting, auditing, and business law.

1.4 Attestation Standards

The standards used to conduct audit as well as other attest services provide guidance to practitioners and relative assurance to users of these services. The AICPA adopted these standards in a pronouncement entitled "Statements on Standards for Attestation Engagements." The attestation standards embrace generally accepted auditing standards, but cover all attest engagements. Generally accepted auditing standards (GAAS) are the basis for the auditing procedures used for the audit of the financial statements.

1.4.1 Absence of Auditing Standards in Non-Audit Engagements

In non-audit attest services, the practitioner identifies the assertion evaluated in the report. The engagement is contingent on the belief that the assertion is capable of evaluation against reasonable criteria whether established by a recognized body or agreed upon. In the latter case, the report on the engagement should contain a statement limiting its use to the parties who have agreed upon such criteria or procedures.

The audit engagement is limited to the expression of an opinion on the fairness of financial statements in accordance with generally accepted accounting principles.

1.4.2 Absence of Attestation Standards in Audit Engagements

In audit attest services, the auditor must obtain a sufficient understanding of the internal control structure in order to determine the nature, timing, and extent of tests to be performed. Also, the auditor's report shall either contain an expression of opinion regarding the financial statements, taken as a whole, or an assertion to the effect that an opinion cannot be expressed. Other attest engagements do not require an understanding of internal control or permit a disclaimer of opinion.

1.5 Generally Accepted Auditing Standards

The audit attest function follows auditing standards, collectively referred to as generally accepted auditing standards (GAAS), which are the basic guidelines for the performance of an audit of financial statements. The Auditing Standards Board (ASB) of the American Institute of Certified Public Accountants (AICPA) promulgated these standards and issues "Statements on Auditing Standards" (SASs) which provide application and interpretation guidelines of these standards.

The basic framework for conduct of an audit consists of ten generally accepted auditing standards, which are segregated into three categories: General Standards, Standards of Field Work, and Standards of Reporting.

1.5.1 General Standards

1. *Technical competence,* e.g., adequate technical training and proficiency.

2. *Independence* in mental attitude.

3. *Due professional care* in the performance of the audit and the preparation of the report.

1.5.2 Standards of Field Work

1. Adequate *planning* of the audit and proper *supervision* of assistants.

2. Sufficient understanding of the *internal control* structure for planning the audit and determining the nature, timing, and extent of tests to be performed.

3. Sufficient, competent *evidence* through inspection, observation, inquiries, and confirmations to afford a reasonable basis for an opinion on the financial statements.

1.5.3 Standards of Reporting

1. *Conformity with GAAP.* Presentation of the financial statements in accordance with generally accepted accounting principles.

2. *Consistency of application of GAAP.* Identification of inconsistent application of GAAP of current period vs. preceding period.

3. *Adequacy of disclosure.* Assumption that disclosure is reasonably adequate unless otherwise stated in the report.

4. *Expression of an opinion and indication of character of the examination.* Inclusion in the report of an opinion or reasons for a disclaimer and clear-cut indication of the character of the examination and the degree of responsibility of the auditor.

1.5.4 Auditing Standards vs. Auditing Procedures

Auditing standards are the authoritative guidelines for measuring the quality of performance of an audit. These standards describe the broad rules relating to professional characteristics of the auditor and the means for gathering of evidence and reporting audit results. The auditing procedures follow the spirit or essence of the auditing standards and are the specific steps that auditors use to gather evidence.

1.6 Auditor's Opinions

Procedures or steps taken to comply with generally accepted auditing standards lead the auditor to one of four opinions:

1.6.1 Unqualified Opinion

The auditor followed generally accepted auditing standards and believed the financial statements were presented fairly, in all material respects, in conformity with generally accepted accounting principles. The report, in this case, is generally referred to as the auditor's standard report.

Certain circumstances which do not have an impact on the auditors unqualified opinions, may require the auditor to modify the standard unqualified report. These circumstances addressed in an explanatory paragraph are as follows:

1. Reference to other auditors.
2. Emphasis of a matter.
3. Justified departure from GAAP.
4. Inconsistent application of GAAP.
5. Existence of uncertainties.

1.6.2 Qualified Opinion

In this type of opinion, either the auditor was unable to follow generally accepted auditing standards or believes the financial statements are presented fairly, except for some qualification or deficiency. A scope restriction, whether imposed by the client or circumstances, will lead to a qualified opinion, e.g., failure to observe the beginning inventory. Also, a departure by the client from GAAP will also lead to a qualified opinion, e.g., less than full disclosure.

1.6.3 Disclaimer of Opinion

A disclaimer means, in effect, that the auditor is unable to establish whether or not the financial statements are presented fairly. This type of opinion results from a very material scope restriction, including major uncertainties. Accordingly, the auditor does not express an opinion.

1.6.4 Adverse Opinion

The opposite of a unqualified opinion, an adverse opinion states that the financial statements are not presented fairly. The only basis for such an opinion is a very material departure from GAAP, e.g., use of fair values instead of book value for valuation of assets.

Clearly, materiality (i.e., the significance/pervasiveness of a problem) determines whether a qualified or a disclaimer of opinion should be issued in the case of a scope limitation, or whether a qualified or an adverse opinion should be issued in the case of a departure from GAAP.

1.7 Organizations Influencing the Accounting Profession

Various public and private organizations have an influence on the practice of auditing.

1. The Securities and Exchange Commission (SEC) is a federal agency that regulates the issuance and trading of securities and also promulgates accounting standards to be followed by public companies. All public companies are required to file annual audited financial statements with the SEC.

2. The American Institute of Certified Public Accountants is a national voluntary organization that issues professional standards, including a code of professional conduct and other authoritative pronouncements constituting GAAS. It also prepares and grades the CPA examination.

3. The Financial Accounting Standards Board (FASB) is the body designated by the AICPA as having the authority to issue generally accepted accounting principles (GAAP). Therefore, the Statements and Interpretations of the FASB carry the substantial support required for general acceptance by the profession. Other FASB publications also affect accounting practice.

4. The State boards of public accounting regulate public

accounting practice within a state. They grant and may revoke certificates or licenses.

5. State societies are voluntary organizations of CPAs within the various states. These groups represent the interests of their members in all professional matters.

6. The General Accounting Office (GAO) conducts audits of executive branches of the government and, thereby, establishes that government programs are being carried out according to federal regulations.

CHAPTER 2

AUDIT REPORTS

2.1 Auditor's Standard Report

When the auditor has no qualifications or reservations concerning the audit or the financial statements and no need to explain any matter regarding the financial statements and these statements are presented fairly in conformity with generally accepted accounting principles, the auditor renders an unqualified opinion in a standard format—i.e., the auditor's standard report. The report reads as follows:

The Independent Auditors' Standard Report (Title)

To the Stockholders of X Company (Addressee)

(Introductory Paragraph)

We have audited the accompanying balance sheet of X Company as of December 31, 19XX, and the related statements of income, retained earnings, and cash flows for the year then ended. These financial statements are the responsibility of the Company's management. Our responsibility is to express an opinion on these financial statements based on our audit.

(Scope Paragraph)

We conducted our audit in accordance with generally accepted auditing standards. Those standards require that we plan and perform the audit to obtain reasonable assurance about whether the financial statements are free of material misstatements. An audit includes examining, on a test basis, evidence supporting the amounts and disclosures in the financial statements. An audit also includes assessing the accounting principles used and significant estimates made by management, as well as evaluating the overall financial statement presentation. We believe that our audit provides a reasonable basis for our opinion.

(Opinion Paragraph)

In our opinion, the financial statements referred to above present fairly, in all material respects, the financial position of X Company as of December 31, 19XX, and the results of its operations and its cash flows for the year then ended in conformity with generally accepted accounting principles.

(Signature)

Date

2.1.1 Composition of the Auditor's Standard Report

The auditor's standard report should be composed as follows:

1. Title - It should contain the word "independent."
2. Addressee of the Report - It should be addressed to the company or stockholders or board of directors of the company whose financial statements are being audited.
3. Three paragraphs - An introductory, a scope, and an opinion paragraph.
4. Signature - The manual or printed signature of the CPA or the CPA firm.
5. Date - The date of the last day of audit work in the field.

2.1.2 Introductory, Scope, and Opinion Paragraphs

The first or introductory paragraph clarifies the responsibilities of management and the auditors. It points out that management bears primary responsibility for the financial statements (including the related footnotes since they are considered an integral part of the financial statements), while the auditor's responsibility is the expression of an opinion on the financial statements.

The second or scope paragraph states that the auditors conducted the audit in accordance with generally accepted auditing standards and describes the nature of the audit. It points out that an audit provides reasonable (but not absolute) assurance that the financial statements do not contain material misstatements, and that the scope of the audit procedures used provide a reasonable basis for the auditor's opinion.

The third or opinion paragraph indicates the auditor's professional judgment (rather than an absolute guarantee), regarding the fair presentation of the financial statements—an opinion which is unqualified, qualified, adverse, or a disclaimer of opinion.

2.2 Types of Opinions

The auditor expresses one of four opinions as a result of the audit:

Unqualified Opinion. This is a favorable opinion without any qualifications or reservations. It may follow the standard form (presented previously) or a modified form that includes explanatory language for certain circumstances (explained later).

Qualified Opinion. This is a favorable opinion with one or more qualifications or reservations. It states, in effect, that except for certain circumstances the financial statements, taken as a whole, are presented fairly in conformity with generally accepted accounting principles. The circumstances which lead to a qualified opinion include a limitation on the scope of the auditor's examination or an unjustified departure from generally accepted accounting principles.

Adverse Opinion. This is an unfavorable opinion which asserts that the financial statements are not presented fairly in conformity with generally accepted accounting principles. This opinion is expressed in situations where departures from generally accepted accounting principles are so material that the financial statements, viewed as a whole, are deemed misleading.

Disclaimer of Opinion. This, in effect, is the nonexpression of an opinion. It states that because of a material limitation on the scope of

10

the auditor's examination, or a lack of auditor independence, or significant uncertainties, the auditors do not have an adequate basis for expressing an opinion.

2.2.1 Unqualified Opinion

The unqualified opinion, whether in the standard or modified form, fulfills the following four reporting standards:

1. Conformity with GAAP. The unqualified opinion states that the financial statements are presented in accordance with generally accepted accounting principles.
2. Consistency of application of GAAP. The unqualified opinion implies consistency of the application of GAAP and specifically identifies any change in the application of such principles.
3. Adequacy of disclosure. Although the unqualified opinion does not make reference to any financial statement disclosures, it does imply that they are reasonably adequate.
4. Expression of an opinion and indication of the character of the examination. The unqualified opinion contains (a) an expression of opinion regarding the fairness of the presentation of the financial statements taken as a whole and (b) a clear-cut indication that the auditor has performed an audit and taken responsibility for the opinion rendered.

2.2.2 Explanatory Language Added to the Auditor's Standard Report

Sometimes the auditor is somewhat uncomfortable with the standard form and because of certain circumstances feels compelled to add explanatory language to the unqualified opinion. The explanation, which becomes a fourth paragraph, draws attention to certain circumstances leading to modified wording of the standard report.

At times, an auditor relies on another auditor/CPA firm to perform part of the audit, especially when other branches, divisions, or subsidiaries are geographically distant from the client company. The auditor of the client company may decide to rely on the work of the other auditor/CPA firm rather than perform the audit of the outlying parts of an entity.

When multiple auditors participate in an engagement, the auditor/CPA firm which does the majority of the audit work becomes the principal auditor and issues the audit opinion for the combined entity.

The principal auditor has three basic alternatives in wording the report.

1. Omit reference to the other auditors. In this case, the auditor assumes full responsibility for the other auditors' work, based on knowledge of the competence of the other auditors and confidence in the quality of their work.

2. Make reference to the other auditors. If the auditor notes in the report the division of responsibility for the audit engagement among the participating CPA firms, this reference, in effect, is tantamount to sharing responsibility for the audit work with the other auditors.

3. Render a qualified opinion. Where the principal auditor does not wish to rely on the other auditors, permission may be requested to audit the part of the company audited by the other auditors. If refused, the auditor may issue a qualified opinion or disclaimer, based on a scope limitation.

In addition, the auditor may wish to add an explanatory paragraph in which details regarding a particular aspect of the financial statements, such as related party transactions, changes in accounting estimates, and changes in operating conditions, may be emphasized. Such an explanatory paragraph may be placed either before or after the opinion paragraph, and does not change the unqualified nature of the auditor's opinion.

Occasionally, the auditors may endorse a departure from generally accepted accounting principles when such a departure leads to a more appropriate presentation and, if otherwise, the financial statements would be misleading. An explanatory paragraph, either before or after the opinion paragraph, justifies the departure under Rule 203 of the AICPA Code of Professional Conduct and requires the auditors to disclose and justify such departure. Any departure from GAAP is indicated in an explanatory paragraph which may be placed either before or after the opinion paragraph. Again, such an explanatory paragraph does not change the unqualified nature of the auditor's opinion.

If a change in accounting principles or in the method of their application has a material effect on the comparability of the company's financial statements, the auditor refers to a footnote which describes the nature, justification, and the effect of the change. Changes between acceptable principles do not require qualification of the auditor's opinions but do require modification of the unqualified opinion with the adding of an explanatory paragraph placed after the scope paragraph. A change which the auditor cannot justify and where the effect on the financial statements is highly material requires the auditor to issue an adverse opinion.

Like contingencies, **uncertainties** are transactions that may or may not occur depending on some future events, but whereas contingencies are susceptible to reasonable estimation, uncertainties are not. Any uncertainties should be described by the auditor in an explanatory paragraph which is placed following the opinion paragraph of the standard report.

A special type of uncertainty relates to the ability of a company to continue as a going concern. The auditors look at the entity's cash flows, loan deposits, and other pertinent data to determine the likelihood of continuation of the firm. Accordingly, if the auditor concludes that continuation of the company is in substantial doubt an explanatory paragraph after the opinion paragraph explains this uncertainty. This explanation does not affect the unqualified nature of the auditor's report.

2.3 Effects of Materiality

The auditors can issue an unqualified report only in the absence of any material deficiencies in either auditing or accounting standards. Materiality refers to qualitative or quantitative characteristics that are sufficiently important to influence decisions made by reasonable users of financial statements.

The degree of materiality influences the type of opinion which the auditor renders. In general, deficiencies which are immaterial do not affect the opinion, those which are material lead to a qualified opinion and those which are significantly material result in an adverse opinion or disclaimer of opinion, depending on whether the matter relates to accounting or auditing standards.

2.3.1 Material and Highly Material Scope Limitations

A scope limitation may arise when the auditors cannot perform a usual audit procedure, due to circumstances or client restrictions. Sometimes the auditor may be able to perform alternate procedures to satisfy audit requirements.

The auditor should issue a qualified opinion when the scope limitation is material and no alternate auditing procedures are available. However, when the scope limitation is highly material, the auditor should disclaim an opinion on the basis that an audit lacking sufficient scope does not conform to generally accepted auditing standards, and thereby precludes the expression of an opinion.

2.3.2 Material and Significantly Material Departures from GAAP

Unless justified, departures from generally accepted accounting principles require a qualified opinion if the effect is material and an adverse opinion, if significantly material. Departures from GAAP include inadequate financial statement disclosure, since such inadequacy violates the full disclosure accounting principle.

2.3.3 Qualified Opinion

The phrase "except for" indicates a qualification of the auditor's opinion and implies a deficiency explained in a separate explanatory paragraph before the opinion paragraph. The opinion paragraph consists of an appropriate qualifying phrase and makes reference to the explanatory paragraph.

14

A qualified opinion should be issued when the exception pertains to a material departure from GAAP, or a material unjustified change in accounting principle, or a material scope limitation imposed by circumstances or the client.

2.3.4 Adverse Opinion

An adverse opinion is the opposite of an unqualified opinion. It states that the financial statements do not present fairly the financial position, results of operations and cash flows of the client, in conformity with generally accepted accounting principles. A significantly material departure from GAAP or unjustifiable change in GAAP leads to an unfair presentation of the financial statements and is, in fact, the only reason for the issuance of an adverse opinion.

2.3.5 Disclaimer of Opinion

A disclaimer of opinion states that the auditor does not express an opinion on the financial statements. The auditor uses disclaimers where the audit has been subject to:

1. Significantly material scope limitations.
2. Existence of significant uncertainties.

Additionally, the auditor also disclaims an opinion when engaged to perform compilations or review accounting services.

An expression of opinion on specific financial statement items, such as cash, accounts receivable, or accounts payable, following an adverse opinion or a disclaimer of opinion is no longer permissible because it tends to weaken the effect of an adverse opinion or disclaimer of opinion.

CHAPTER 3

PROFESSIONAL ETHICS

3.1 Characteristics of a Profession

Whether it be law, medicine, engineering, or auditing, each profession has common characteristics, namely:

1. Responsibility to others besides the parties which have engaged the professional.
2. A complex body of knowledge constantly undergoing change.
3. Rigorous qualifications which generally include obtaining licensure to practice the profession.
4. Willingness to accept and abide by ethical standards of professional conduct.

3.2 AICPA Code of Professional Conduct

The AICPA restructured its *Code of Professional Conduct* effective in 1988. The restructured *Code* consists of a section in principles which are broad definitions of concepts and rules which are enforceable applications of the principles.

Interpretations of rules provide clarification of the rules: The Senior Technical Committees of the AICPA, e.g., the Auditing Standards Board interprets rules applicable to auditing while the Professional Ethics Division Executive Committee deals with matters that apply to professional activities.

The AICPA also issues *Ethics Rulings* which explain the application of the rules and interpretations to specific factual circumstances involving professional ethics.

3.2.1 Principles

Principles are statements of the profession's responsibilities to its clients, the public, and to colleagues. CPAs must serve the needs of their clients in keeping with the interest of outside parties in their services and also must strive to enhance the art of accounting.

3.2.2 Responsibilities

CPAs have responsibilities to their clients, their employers, colleagues, and to the general public. A professional attitude and respect toward all these interests should be part of the CPA's approach to resolution of inevitable conflicts.

3.2.3 Public Interest

In regard to accounting services, the public consists of clients, creditors, government, employers, and investors. Conflicting pressures from these groups should not influence the judgment of CPAs. They should demonstrate integrity, objectivity, independence, and due care in the performance of their services.

3.2.4 Integrity, Objectivity, and Independence

CPAs should strive to perform their services with integrity, objectivity, and independence. Integrity means absolute honesty and forthrightness. Objectivity refers to freedom from bias or conflicts of interest. Independence applies not only in fact but in appearance.

3.2.5 Due Care

CPAs should observe due care in the performance of their services. Due care describes the conscientious attention to technical and ethical standards, as well as continual endeavors for improvement in competence and quality of services in order to discharge professional responsibility in the best possible manner.

3.2.6 Scope and Nature of Services

CPAs must determine whether or not to provide specific services in individual circumstances. Factors to be considered include:

1. Knowledge required to provide services in a competent manner.
2. Freedom from conflict of interest (i.e., independence).
3. Availability of capable staff.
4. Integrity of prospective client.

3.3 Rules of Conduct

The Rules of Conduct emanate from the principles and are, in fact, enforceable applications of the principles. The by-laws of the AICPA require that members adhere to the Rules of Professional Conduct and justify any departure from the Rules or otherwise face disciplinary actions and exposure to litigation.

3.3.1 Independence - Rule 101

Independence is the single most important Rule of Conduct. Many of the other Rules are simply variations of this overriding theme.

Basically, the rule on independence states that certain relationships of CPAs with clients constitute a violation of independence. These relationships should not exist during the period of a professional engagement or at the time of expressing an opinion if they involve:

1. A direct or material indirect investment in the enterprise.
2. A fiduciary position where a trust or estate has agreed to make a direct or material indirect investment in the enterprise.

3. A joint closely held business investment with the enterprise or officer, director or principle stockholders where the investment is material to one party or the other.

4. A loan to or from the enterprise except for loans made under normal lending conditions and not material to the net worth of the borrower, home mortgages, and other secured loans, not guaranteed by a CPA firm.

In addition, independence is impaired if during the period of the engagement or at the time of expressing an opinion, the CPA or firm acts as an employee, including promoter, underwriter, director, officer, or voting trustee, including trustee of any pension or profit sharing trust of the enterprise.

Situations which impair independence include:

1. *Long overdue fees* owed by a client to a CPA firm placing the client and firm in a debtor-creditor relationship.

2. *Litigation* between the client and the auditor.

3. Appearance of *excessive friendliness* between the CPA and the client.

Almost as important as independence in fact is the appearance of independence. An overly friendly association of individuals on both sides involved in attestation engagements or an exchange of expensive gifts may cause a wrong perception of a lack of independence by observers. Other factors to consider in regard to independence include:

1. Applicability of the rule to various services. The rule of independence applies to auditing and other attestation services but does not apply to management consulting, tax, and accounting services.

2. Independence of partners and staff. In auditing and other attestation services, all partners (or stockholders), all managerial employees in the office assigned to the engagement, and all professional staff personally participating in the engagement must be independent.

3. Effect of relatives on independence. Rules of attribution apply to a CPA's spouse, dependent children, or relatives so that any direct financial interest impairs inde-

pendence. Only a material indirect financial interest affects independence of other close relatives.

3.3.2 Integrity and Objectivity - Rule 102

In the performance of any professional service, CPAs shall maintain objectivity and integrity, shall be free of conflicts of interest and shall not knowingly misrepresent facts or subordinate their judgment to others.

This rule recognizes the considerable pressures CPAs face in attest engagements where clients, employers, and others may attempt to influence their judgment. CPAs must always remember that they are ultimately responsible for their decisions.

3.3.3 General Standards - Rule 201

CPAs must comply with certain standards:

1. Applying professional competence.
2. Exercising due professional care.
3. Planning and supervision.
4. Obtaining sufficient relevant data.

These standards, similar to some of the auditing standards, are applicable to all CPAs. If unable to meet the standard of competence, CPAs attempt to acquire the required competence before they refer the engagement to someone else.

3.3.4 Compliance with Standards - Rule 202

CPAs must follow standards promulgated by bodies designated by the AICPA council. Such bodies are the Auditing Standards Board for auditing services, the Management Advisory Services Executive Committee for consulting services, the Accounting and Review Services Committee for unaudited financial statement services and the Financial Accounting Standards Board for generally accepted accounting principles (GAAP).

3.3.5 Accounting Principles - Rule 203

CPAs express an opinion on financial statements on the basis of conformity with GAAP. If the statements do not conform with GAAP, the departure, if justified on the basis that compliance would be misleading, would not preclude an expression of an unqualified opinion.

3.3.6 Confidential Client Information - Rule 301

CPAs in public practice shall not disclose any confidential client information without the specific consent of the client.

Exceptions to the rule require disclosure under:

1. Rules 202 and 203 relating to compliance with professional standards.
2. Subpoena or summons requiring testimony in a court of law.
3. Review of CPAs professional practice by the AICPA or state society of CPAs.
4. Inquiry by a recognized, investigative or disciplinary body.

Confidentiality is characteristic of other professions - law, medicine, the clergy - but, whereas information divulged to members of these professions is privileged, CPAs must disclose confidential information when required by court order (except in certain states).

3.3.7 Contingent Fees - Rule 302

CPAs cannot charge fees contingent on their findings or on the results of their services when the engagement requires independence. Exceptions to this rule are fees:

1. Fixed by courts or other public authorities or in tax matters.
2. Based on the results of judicial proceedings or the findings of governmental agencies.

A recently interpreted agreement between the AICPA and the Federal Trade Commission allows contingent fees and commissions for services to non-attest clients.

3.3.8 Acts Discreditable - Rule 501

CPAs shall not commit an act discreditable to the profession. A felony would be a violation of this rule. Other acts which would violate this rule include:

1. Discriminatory employment practices.
2. Failure to return client's records.
3. Signing a false or misleading opinion.
4. Intentional misrepresentation of client's financial statements or records.

3.3.9 Advertising - Rule 502

CPAs in public practice shall not seek clients by advertising or other forms of solicitation in a manner that is false, misleading, or deceptive. Coercion, overreaching, and harassment are among the unacceptable forms of solicitation.

Unethical advertising includes advertising which:

1. Creates false or unjustified expectations of future results.
2. Implies the ability to influence a court or other official body.
3. Makes unfavorable comparisons with other CPAs.

3.3.10 Commissions - Rule 503

CPAs in public practice are not allowed to take (nor give) a commission for the referral of a potential client from (to) others when they perform attest services for the client referred.

As mentioned earlier, the AICPA and the FTC have agreed to allow commissions and contingent fees for services to non-attest clients.

3.3.11 Form of Practice and Name - Rule 504   505 in book

CPAs may practice public accounting only in the form of a proprietorship, a partnership, or a professional corporation whose characteristics conform to specific requirements.

The intent of this rule is to assure that CPAs carry on their practices in a professional manner and in accordance with the spirit of the Code of Professional Conduct. The firm name must not be misleading. It cannot imply a partnership if the firm is, in fact, a sole proprietorship. Nor can the firm designate itself as "Members of the American Institute of Certified Public Accountants" unless all its partners or shareholders are members of the Institute.

If the practice is under the aegis of a professional corporation, the stockholders must all be individuals authorized to practice public accounting. The professional corporation must also carry sufficient professional liability insurance to protect the public.

CHAPTER 4

LEGAL LIABILITY

4.1 Legal Relationships

Legal liability of auditors depends on whether they have:

1. Violated any laws governing the profession (common and statutory law).

2. Performed their work in a negligent or fraudulent manner (ordinary or gross negligence and fraud).

3. Caused clients or other parties to suffer damages (privity, primary and foreseen or foreseeable beneficiaries).

4. Unsuccessfully upheld their lack of guilt (burden of proof).

4.1.1 Common and Statutory Law

Common law is evolutionary law since it did not originate from written statutes but developed through court decisions, some of which go back to old English law of several centuries ago.

Statutory law is legislative or written law since it results from passage of legislation by a governmental unit, such as the federal securities acts and state blue-sky laws which regulate the issuance and trading of securities. Common law rules in cases involving nonpublic clients. Either common law or statutory law may support a law suit brought against an auditor by a stockholder of a public company. In such cases, the client or other injured party is likely to be more successful under statutory law.

4.1.2 Ordinary or Gross Negligence and Fraud

To be found liable, a client or other injured party must prove violation of an auditor's responsibility, i.e., negligence or fraud.

Ordinary negligence represents a lack of reasonable care in the performance of one's duty. In accounting, ordinary negligence means failure to apply the professional standards that ordinarily competent auditors would have applied in the same or other similar circumstances.

Gross negligence constitutes the lack of even slight care in the performance of one's duty. In accounting, gross negligence implies extreme or reckless disregard or the omission under practically all circumstances of the professional standards usually exercised by practitioners.

Whereas ordinary and gross negligence do not involve intent, fraud is intentional. Fraud is the false representation of a material fact known to be untrue or made with reckless indifference as to whether the fact is true.

Constructive or technical fraud does not involve intentional misrepresentation. However, gross negligence is equivalent to constructive or technical fraud since it involves complete indifference as to whether a fact is true or not.

4.1.3 Privity, Primary and Foreseen or Foreseeable Beneficiaries

Privity is the relationship between parties to a contract or the contractual relationship between the auditor and client for the performance of professional services.

A third party beneficiary is a party either named or identified in a contract or intended by the parties in privity to have certain rights and benefits under the contract. Such a third party beneficiary has a primary beneficiary relationship and has recourse against auditors similar to those of clients.

Since the 1960s third parties not specifically known to the auditor and thus not having a primary beneficiary relationship have been successful in liability cases against auditors. The courts have construed certain parties suffering a loss from the reliance on audited financial statements of the auditor's client as foreseen or foreseeable parties.

Foreseen parties are parties known to, or reasonably expected to be known to, the auditor as placing reliance on the financial statements and the auditor's report (for example, banks).

Foreseeable parties are parties not reasonably expected to be known to the auditor, but those who may reasonably be expected to have access to and place reliance on the financial statements and the auditor's report (for example, vendors or customers).

4.1.4 Burden of Proof

Burden of proof denotes whether the plaintiff must prove the guilt of the auditor as a defendant or whether the auditor as the defendant must prove the lack of guilt.

Under common law, the plaintiff must demonstrate the:

1. Misleading nature of the financial statements.
2. Damages suffered.
3. Negligence or fraud or breach of contract on the part of the auditor.
4. Reliance on the financial statements.

Under statutory law, the auditor as defendant must demonstrate the:

1. Exercise of due diligence or good faith, depending on the applicable statute.
2. Contributory negligence on the part of the plaintiff.

4.2 Common Law Liability

Common law applies to negligence or fraud cases for nonpublic companies or public companies where the federal securities or state blue-sky laws are not an issue. The plaintiff under common law can be the client, third party beneficiary, and other third parties and must prove damages or loss, auditor negligence, and proximate cause or damages attributable to the auditor's negligence. The degree of negligence can be ordinary, except in certain jurisdictions where it must be gross negligence.

4.2.1 Liability to Client

The client, in a suit against the auditor, must prove damages resulting from the auditor's negligence. As defendants, the auditors must demonstrate lack of negligence on their part or contributory negligence by the client. In some jurisdictions allocation of damages may follow comparative negligence or the extent of fault between the two parties.

On the question of confidentiality, CPAs should insist on complete and full disclosure in the financial statements of all events which may affect their opinion. This rule applies even if the client has committed an illegal act as long as it does not bear on the auditor's opinion.

Rule 301 of the Code of Professional Conduct states that CPAs must not disclose confidential client information without the specific consent of the client. This rule does not affect the auditor's obligation to comply with a validly issued and enforceable subpoena or summons. If damages to the client result from the auditor's testimony in court, the client will have no basis for a lawsuit.

Apart from legal liability and confidentiality, the auditor also has a limited responsibility for the detection and reporting of errors and irregularities. Errors are unintentional mistakes or omissions in financial statements, including mistakes in the application of generally accepted accounting principles. Irregularities are intentional misstatements or omissions in the financial statements or misrepresentation of assets.

SAS 53 requires that auditors design their audit to provide reasonable assurance of detecting errors and irregularities that are material to the financial statements and report irregularities of any consequence to the audit committee of the client's board of directors. Despite their efforts, the auditors may not detect material errors and irregularities and if a material misstatement or omission finds its way into the financial statements, the auditors are not automatically at fault.

4.2.2 Liability to Third Parties

Unlike the auditors' liability to the client, their liability to third parties varies from one jurisdiction to another. Under common law, the client must prove only ordinary negligence, but as a result of various legal cases, third parties, in certain jurisdictions, must prove gross negligence and, in other jurisdictions, need prove only ordinary negligence.

The **Ultramares Case** *(Ultramares vs. Touche)* established the precedent that the auditors could not be held liable to unidentified third parties for *ordinary* negligence, but only held liable for *gross* negligence.

Other cases reaffirmed the Ultramares precedent, for example, the case of *Credit Alliance vs. Arthur Andersen.*

The **Rusch Factors Case** *(Rusch Factors vs. Levin)* extended the liability of the auditors for ordinary negligence to foreseen parties. The court in this case held that the plaintiff in the Ultramares case was a foreseeable rather than a foreseen party.

The **Rosenblum Case** *(Rosenblum vs. Adler)* found that auditors can be held liable for ordinary negligence to foreseeable third parties. Whether unidentified third parties can bring suit for ordinary or gross negligence on the basis of being foreseen or foreseeable beneficiaries under the contract between the client and the auditor, depends on which legal precedent prevails in the particular jurisdiction—Ultramares or Rosenblum.

4.3 Statutory Law Liability

Statutory Law applies to negligence or fraud cases for public companies under the federal securities or state blue-sky laws and both nonpublic and public companies under other written laws such as the Racketeer Influenced and Corrupt Organizations Act (RICO). The principal laws auditors must follow are the Securities Act of 1933 and the Securities Exchange Act of 1934.

4.3.1 Securities Act of 1933

The 1933 Act requires a company intending to offer its securities for sale to the public to file a registration statement with the Securities and

Exchange Commission (SEC). The registration statement includes audited financial statements. The company filing the registration statement and its auditors may be held liable to the initial purchasers of the securities in the event the registration statement contains material distortions.

4.3.2 Securities Exchange Act of 1934

The Securities Exchange Act of 1934 requires public companies to file audited annual financial statements with the SEC. The company filing the audited statements and its auditors may be held liable to anyone who buys or sells the company's securities in the event the financial statements contain material distortions.

4.3.3 Liability Under the 1933 and 1934 Acts

The 1933 Act provides that third-party investors—those who bought a security on its initial offering—have the right to recover losses caused by the auditors' ordinary negligence as well as gross negligence or fraud. The third-party investors have a prima facie case and need not prove that they relied on the financial statements.

The 1934 Act provides that third-party investors—those who bought or sold the security at any time—have the right to recover losses caused by the auditors' gross negligence (as well as fraud) as established by Section 18(a) of the 1934 Act. In some court decisions, auditors have been held liable for losses caused by ordinary negligence.

Losses under both 1933 and 1934 Acts are the differences between the purchase price of the security and the market price at the time of the suit or the sales price, if the security was sold.

4.3.4 Auditors' Defenses Under the 1933 and 1934 Acts

The burden of proof is on the auditors to show that factors other than the auditor's negligence caused the third-party losses or, in other words, that their negligence was not the cause of the losses. For the 1933 Act, the auditors must prove that they exercised due diligence and were not negligent or that their negligence was not the proximate cause of the plaintiff's losses. For the 1934 Act, the auditors must prove that they acted in good faith and had no knowledge that the financial statements were false or misleading.

4.3.5 Lawsuits Brought Under the Securities Acts

McKesson and Robbins Case. As a result of this famous case, the SEC required the auditor's report to make reference to the conduct of the audit in accordance with generally accepted auditing standards. The AICPA also required that auditors gather independent and external evidence on accounts receivable and inventory.

Hochfelder vs. Ernst. This landmark case contracted rather than expanded the auditors' liability to third parties. The U.S. Supreme Court decided that auditors could not be held liable under the Securities Exchange Act of 1934 for ordinary negligence.

Continental Vending Case (United States vs. Simon). In a corollary case, three members of the CPA firm that audited Continental's Financial Statements were convicted of criminal fraud (later pardoned) on the basis of gross negligence. Both Securities Acts include provisions for criminal charges against persons violating provisions of the Acts.

Escott vs. BarChris. This case demonstrated the application of the 1933 Securities Act in bringing suit against auditors for ordinary negligence. As a result of this case, auditors must place greater emphasis on subsequent events (post balance sheet) procedures and understanding the client's business and internal control.

Equity Funding Case. This case illustrated the importance of proper documentation to show support for evidence and close security for working papers to insure confidentiality of testing. It also revealed how a massive fraud could be unnoticed when due care is lacking.

4.3.6 Liability for Accounting and Review Services

Not only are auditors liable under common law and statutory law for audits, but they are also liable under these laws for other accounting services, such as income tax work and compilations or reviews of unaudited financial statements. Compilation refers to preparation of financial statements from the client's records while a review consists of limited investigative procedures. Both of these accounting services lead to a disclaimer of opinion. CPAs acting as accountants have an obligation to exercise due professional care and may be liable under common law for losses to third parties resulting from ordinary or gross negligence.

1136 Tenant's Case Corporation vs. Rothenburg Case. This case emphasized that the auditors must exercise due professional care in a non-attest engagement and be alert to suspicious evidence. More important, the case demonstrated the need for an engagement letter clearly stating the nature and scope of the proposed work.

4.3.7 Racketeer Influenced and Corrupt Organization Act

This act, referred to as RICO, passed in 1970 by Congress, is an anti-racketeering law which included crimes such as mail fraud and fraud in the sale of securities. RICO provides for triple damages to be awarded the plaintiff and has been the basis of suits alleging that the auditors knew or should have known of material misstatements or omissions in the financial statements.

CHAPTER 5

ENGAGEMENT PLANNING

5.1   Planning Process

The first standard of field work of the generally accepted auditing standards states:

"The work is to be adequately planned and assistants, if any, are to be properly supervised."

In planning an audit, an auditor should obtain a knowledge of the client's business, discuss preliminary arrangements with the client, and develop an audit strategy. Throughout the planning process, the auditors must take into account materiality and audit risk.

5.2   Knowledge of the Client's Business

Knowledge of the client's business is important because it may have an impact on the accounting methods of the company. The nature of the business affects revenue recognition and matching of expenses, as well as the recognition or deferral of assets and liabilities. Such questions differ between retail enterprises, construction contractors, and manufacturing companies.

The auditor's knowledge of the client's business should include:

1. Understanding of the client's organizational structure, accounting policies and procedures, capital structure, product lines, and methods of production and distribution.

2. Familiarity with matters affecting the industry within which the client operates, including economic conditions and financial trends, inherent types of business risk, governmental regulations, changes in technology, and widely used accounting methods. Such a knowledge of the client's business environment permits the auditor to be in a position to evaluate the appropriateness of the accounting principles and the reasonableness of the many estimates and assumptions used in the financial statements.

3. Analytical procedures or comparisons of financial statement balances and ratios for the year under audit with the prior year, or budgets or the industry.

4. Tour of plant and offices. A tour of the plant and offices of a prospective client will give the auditors some understanding of the location of records, plant layout, manufacturing process, principal products, physical safeguards surrounding inventories and potential problems such as obsolete inventory.

5.2.1 Sources of Knowledge of Client's Business

Knowledge of a particular industry and general economic conditions comes from many sources such as:

1. Inquiries of client management regarding industry conditions, new accounting pronouncements, unusual accounting transactions, and the effects of such information on the entity's financial statements and its production and marketing operations.

2. AICPA audit and accounting guides, trade publications, and governmental agency publications useful in obtaining an orientation in the client's industry.

3. Previous audit reports, annual reports to stockholders, SEC filings, and prior years' tax returns.

5.3   Preliminary Arrangement and Engagement Letter

Before making a commitment for the engagement, the auditor confers with the client to avoid any misunderstandings.

The preliminary understanding with the client becomes the basis of an engagement letter. The engagement letter describes the:

1. Nature, purpose, and scope of the audit.
2. Use of the client's staff.
3. Schedule of work.
4. Fee arrangements.
5. Extent of the verification of the validity of plant and equipment and inventory accounts.

Other accounting services also make use of engagement letters. A written understanding signed by the client and the CPA helps avoid legal problems, such as occurred in the 1136 Tenants vs. Rothenberg case.

5.4   Development of an Audit Strategy

When the completed contract is in hand, an engagement team, composed of the auditors, tax and management consulting personnel meets to develop an audit strategy. This strategy identifies the primary risk areas and considers such matters as indications of:

1. Management tendency to alter financial statements.
2. Reliability of accounting estimates.
3. Efficiency in operating, accounting, or data processing.
4. Adequacy of security over data or assets.

Knowledge of the client's business assists the auditors to plan an approach that results in the most efficient audit. In formulating this approach the auditors make choices involving:

1. Statistical vs. non-statistical sampling.
2. Manual vs. EDP audit techniques.

3. Experience levels of auditors to be used.

4. Use of other auditors for branch locations.

The auditors must also consider carefully the suitable levels of materiality and audit risk.

5.4.1 Materiality

For planning purposes, **materiality** is the auditors preliminary estimate of the smallest amount of misstatement that would probably influence the judgment of a reasonable person relying on the financial statements. In other words, materiality is the maximum error the auditors would be willing to tolerate in the financial statements and still issue a favorable opinion—unqualified or qualified—on the financial statements. The level of materiality is generally a function of:

1. Quantitative factors, the amount of a transaction, including the relationship of a misstatement in one item to other items in the financial statements, such as income before taxes, total assets, total current assets, total stockholder's equity.

2. Qualitative factors, the nature of a transaction, including the probability of illegal transactions or irregularities and violation of loan agreements.

5.4.2 Audit Risk

Audit risk is the possibility that the auditors may accept the financial statements as being fair when, in fact, they contain a material misstatement. The possible acceptance of misleading statements or audit risk consists of three types of risk—inherent risk, control risk, and detection risk. The auditor relies on auditing procedures to uncover material misstatements, but regardless of the nature and extent of the procedures, certainty of detection is not possible; therein lies the risk called detection risk.

The auditing procedures used by the auditor are the result of the auditor's study and evaluation of internal control. Control risk is the possibility that this evaluation will fail to prevent or discover an internal control weakness that may lead to a material misstatement. The evaluation of internal control permits the auditor to assess the effectiveness of the internal control and design the appropriate auditing procedures to lessen detection risk.

Regardless of the failure of control or detection procedures to prevent the acceptance of misleading financial statements, material misstatements will escape detection because of inherent or built-in risk which internal control cannot prevent.

The auditors compare the achieved overall audit risk to the planned audit risk to determine whether to accept the financial statements as fairly presented and not materially misstated.

Inherent risk is the susceptibility to material error in the absence of internal control. Factors causing inherent risk are:

1. Technological obsolescence, leading to over valuation of inventory and productive assets.

2. Lack of management skills and experience, making for inability to solve operational or financial problems.

3. Unfavorable economic conditions, inducing intentional misstatements.

4. Form of ownership providing incentives for tax minimization incentives for closely-held entities and profit maximization techniques for public companies.

Control risk is the probability that the internal control system will not prevent or detect material errors on a timely basis. In planning the audit, the auditor must assess the extent of inherent and control risks for each material financial statement account. Based on the assessment of control risk, the auditor can then design auditing procedures to reduce detection risk to a suitable level.

Detection risk is the probability that material errors not only will escape discovery from the study and evaluation of internal control but also by auditing procedures designed to detect such material misstatements. The auditing procedures will vary inversely with the reliance on the internal control structure or assessment of control risk. The greater this reliance or the lower the assessment of control risk the less auditing procedures the auditor will plan to perform and vice versa.

5.5 Segments of an Audit

The auditors divide the audit work so that it roughly follows four phases, namely:

Phase I or Planning. In this phase the auditor develops an overall audit strategy of the work that needs to be done and then schedules the work either before the balance sheet date or after the balance sheet date.

Phase II or Interim Auditing Work. As much work as possible during the period before the balance sheet date makes for an efficient audit. Such work includes study and evaluation of internal control, review of minutes of meetings, tests of additions or reductions of long-term assets or liabilities.

Phase III or Year-End Audit Work. Procedures which must wait until the completion of the period include observation of physical inventory, count of cash funds, inspection of marketable or investment securities.

Phase IV or Final Audit Work. This phase consists of all audit procedures not previously conducted, including certain procedures subsequent to the balance sheet date and also the preparation and issuance of the audit report.

5.6 Audit Plan

The audit plan written before starting work, is an overview of the engagement, describing the client company and outlining the overall audit strategy. It answers questions on:

1. Characteristics of the client's business.

2. Objectives and scope of the audit, identifying special problems and preliminary estimates of materiality levels.

3. Timing, scheduling, and personnel requirements of the audit work with target dates for completion of procedures.

5.7   Audit Program

The audit program is a detailed listing of the steps that the auditors follow to assess internal control and accumulated evidence on the fairness of the financial statements.

The audit program consists of tests of controls and substantive tests or tests of monetary balances.

5.7.1 Tests of Controls

Tests of controls, formerly called compliance tests, are procedures designed to assess the control risk or whether the internal control system is working as established by the client (i.e., operating effectiveness).

These tests measure the extent to which control procedures are actually in operation and also the propriety of the internal control design. Based on the results of tests of controls, the auditors make an assessment of control risk and determine the extent and nature of substantive tests.

5.7.2 Substantive Tests

Substantive tests are tests of account balances and transactions designed to reduce detection risk, that is, to uncover any material errors in the financial statements. These tests relate to the monetary balances in the financial statements.

CHAPTER 6

INTERNAL CONTROL STRUCTURE IN MANUALLY OPERATED SYSTEMS

6.1 Definition of Internal Control

Internal control is a term that describes the methods and procedures used by a business to carry out its activities or operations. It consists of measures designed to:

1. Safeguard assets from waste and fraud.
2. Promote reliable accounting records.
3. Encourage and measure compliance with company policies.
4. Evaluate the efficiency of operations.

6.1.1 Internal Accounting vs. Internal Administrative Controls

Internal accounting controls relate to controls that affect reported accounting data or those measures concerned with the safeguarding of assets and promoting the reliability of accounting records.

Internal administrative controls relate to controls that affect authorization decisions or those measures concerned with encouraging compliance with company policies and evaluating the efficiency of operations.

6.2 Elements of Internal Control

Internal control has three elements:

1. Control environment or the context within which the measures become operative.

2. Accounting system or the means to assemble, analyze, classify, record, and report an entity's transactions.

3. Control procedures or the policies and methods which provide reasonable assurance of achieving the specific entity objectives.

6.2.1 Control Environment

The control environment reflects the attitudes and actions of management and consists of the factors designed to achieve the entity's policies and procedures. Environmental factors include:

1. Management philosophy and operating style.

2. Organizational structure.

3. Personnel management methods.

4. Forecasting and budgeting system.

5. Internal auditing.

6. Audit committee.

Management may be conservative or aggressive in taking business risks or reporting operating results. Different philosophies or operating styles affect the internal control and may increase control risk.

Organizational structure refers to a plan of organization or the division of authority, responsibilities and duties among the personnel of an entity. A well-designed organizational structure separates responsibilities for:

1. Authorization of transactions.

2. Record keeping for transactions.

3. Execution of the operation.

4. Accountability or custody of assets.

The strength of the internal control depends on such personnel management methods as hiring, training, evaluating, promoting, and compensating employees. Effective policies in these areas will lessen weaknesses in the control environment.

Fidelity bonds, although not a substitute for personnel policies, provide reimbursement for losses attributable to theft or embezzlement by bonded employees and the investigation required for bonding reduces the likelihood of hiring dishonest employees.

A financial forecast or budget provides management with a standard for evaluating actual results and thus serves as an internal control device by:

1. Permitting comparisons of interim actual results with budgeted figures, followed by explanations of all significant variations and timely corrective actions to be taken by responsible individuals.

2. Motivating company personnel to strive for certain goals.

Internal auditing investigates the efficacy and the efficiency of the various departments of a business and thereby serves to appraise the internal control system.

Whereas the external auditor renders an opinion on the fairness of the financial statements, the internal auditor assists management with enhancing the efficiency and effectiveness of the organization. Operational audits performed by internal auditors attempt to evaluate the effect of the existing policies and procedures in attaining these goals.

The audit committee maintains a liaison between the board of directors and the independent or internal auditors. When independent from management and not composed of employees of the company, the audit committee is better able to oversee the internal control structure and to appraise the management of the company.

6.2.2 Accounting System

The accounting system consists of the mechanics for proper recording, processing, and reporting of business transactions. In addition to journals, ledgers, and other records, an accounting system includes:

1. Proper documents.
2. Chart of accounts.
3. Manual of accounting policies and procedures.

Documents perform the function of transmitting information both within and outside an organization. Certain principles dictate the proper design and use of documents, namely:

1. Prenumbered serially to facilitate control.
2. Prepared at or soon after a transaction takes place.
3. Designed for multiple copies to be used for several functions, e.g., recording sales, and receivables, and authorizing shipment.

A chart of accounts is a classified listing of all balance sheet and income statement accounts with an explanation of their purposes and contents. This control device is important because it helps companies control the recording of transactions and reporting of information in a consistent, reliable manner. The chart of accounts contains sufficient information to permit the presentation of financial statements in accordance with generally accepted accounting principles and to assist management decisions.

The manual of accounting policies and procedures define the flow of documents throughout the organization and provide information for adequate record keeping. Clearly stated procedures facilitate proper recording, processing, and reporting of similar transactions, thereby enhancing the reliability of the accounting system.

6.2.3 Control Procedures

The control procedures provide reasonable assurance of achieving the entity's objectives. These procedures include the appropriate segregation of duties as encouraged by the control environment. Such segregation of duties consists of a separate department or person to authorize,

42

initiate, approve, execute, and record each transaction and also a separate department or person to have custody of assets, thereby achieving accountability of assets. A fundamental concept of internal control is that no one department or person should carry out all elements of a transaction from beginning to end. A good example of separation of duties is the division of responsibility between the controller and treasurer. The controller is responsible for accounting or record keeping and has no custodial or operating responsibility. The treasurer has custody of cash, including receipts and disbursements.

The person having custody of an asset should not account for the asset because that person can cover up intentional or unintentional errors by making the records agree with the physical count, e.g., receipt of cash and maintenance of cash records.

The person authorizing a transaction should not have custody of the asset because that person can benefit by authorizing a transaction to obtain access to an asset and then, after obtaining custody, divert the asset for personal gain, e.g., authorization for issuance of a vendor's payment and issuance of the check.

An accounting system may be deficient if one person is responsible for recording a transaction from its origin to its ultimate posting in the general ledger. These circumstances result in a failure to detect unintentional errors and also intentional irregularities.

6.3   Understanding the Internal Control Structure

The second standard of field work requires the auditors to obtain an understanding of internal control, as follows:

> "A sufficient understanding of the internal control structure is to be obtained to plan the audit and to determine the nature, timing, and extent of tests to be performed."

In planning the audit, the auditors must obtain a sufficient understanding of the control environment, accounting system, and control procedures. Such knowledge of the design of the internal control system permits the auditor to:

1. Identify the types of errors in the financial statements.

2. Provide a basis for assessment of control risk or the probability that the internal control will not prevent or detect errors in the financial statements.

3. Design effective substantive tests based on the assessment of control risk. The auditor's understanding of internal control is a major consideration in determining the nature and extent of the substantive tests.

The auditors expect to learn from their understanding of the internal control whether the design of the system makes for effective internal control and, if the design is satisfactory, whether the related internal control measures are actually in use.

6.3.1 Sources of Information on Internal Control Structure

To obtain an understanding of the design of the internal control structure, the auditor:

1. Reviews working papers of prior audits.

2. Makes inquiries of client personnel.

3. Inspects documents and records including organization charts, job descriptions.

4. Observes the company's operations.

The auditor obtains information on implementation of the measures, as designed, from tests of controls. Before tests of controls, the auditor summarizes the information in one or more types of documentation: questionnaire, written narrative, or flowcharts.

An internal control questionnaire asks a series of "yes" or "no" questions about the major transaction cycles. Negative responses indicate potential internal control weakness. The advantages of the internal control questionnaire include broad coverage and ease of use, but its disadvantages include lack of flexibility and a tendency for completion in a mechanical manner.

A written narrative is a description of the major transaction cycles, identifying personnel performing various tasks, documents prepared and records maintained. The advantage of a written narrative is its ability to enhance the understanding of the system, but the time and difficulty of clear exposition also makes this feature a disadvantage.

A flowchart is a symbolic, diagrammatic representation of the client's documents and procedures and their sequential flow in the organization. Flowcharts convey a clear picture of the system, showing the origin of each document or record in the system, its subsequent processing and final disposition and also the separation of duties within the system. The advantage of flowcharts over a questionnaire or narrative is that they provide an easier-to-understand portrayal of the internal control structure. A possible disadvantage of flowcharts is the lack of prominent identification of weaknesses, as would be true of questionnaires or narratives.

6.3.2 Walk-Through Test

Once the auditors have investigated and described the design of the system in the form of a completed questionnaire, written narrative or flowcharts, they follow an example of every document from its origin to its final disposition. This procedure or walk-through test provides a better understanding of the system and helps disclose errors or omissions in the description of the system.

6.3.3 Initial Assessment of Control Risk

Based on the understanding they have acquired of the internal control structure, their description of its design and walk-through testing, the auditors can now apply tests of controls to ascertain whether the system is working as desired. The tests of controls:

1. Identify the types of errors and irregularities that might occur in the financial statements.

2. Evaluate the suitability of the internal control structure to prevent such errors and irregularities.

3. Assess the control risk based on the design of the system and its implementation.

If the initial assessment of control risk is not satisfactory, the auditor may design additional tests of controls to reduce the assessed level of control risk. This approach may succeed in limiting the substantive testing sufficiently to justify the expense of additional tests.

6.3.4 Test of Controls

Thus, tests of controls evaluate the effectiveness of both the design and operation of controls. Such tests focus on compliance with procedures rather than financial statement amounts or completed transactions.

The chief means for application of tests of controls is inspection of documents and reports where a signature or initials or other mark indicates that a procedure has been carried out. The auditors may also test some internal control procedures through observation or inquiries of client personnel.

6.3.5 Final Assessment of Control Risk

After completion of the tests of controls, the auditors make a final assessment of the control risk. This final assessment leads to revisions in the substantive tests—contracted procedures in strong areas and expanded procedures in weak areas. The result of this final assessment, then, is a tailor-made audit program of substantive tests.

6.3.6 Design of Substantive Tests

The substantive tests or tests of financial statement amounts depend on the final assessment of control risk. If an understanding of the internal control is nonexistent or so weak that control risk is assessed at the maximum level, the auditor can forego tests of controls and apply more extensive, be they more costly, substantive tests. The design of these tests must take into account this situation and be detailed and pervasive.

6.3.7 Recommendations for Improvement: Management Letter

The client should receive written, as well, as oral notification of weaknesses in internal control brought to light by the auditor's assessment of the system. The auditor must communicate certain weaknesses, called reportable conditions, to the audit committee of the board of directors. A reportable condition is a significant internal control design or operational weaknesses that could adversely affect the entity's accounting capabilities.

Auditors often discuss both reportable conditions and lesser weaknesses in a management letter. This report can be a valuable source of suggestions to management and can also minimize the auditor's legal liability in the event of financial problems.

CHAPTER 7

INTERNAL CONTROL STRUCTURE IN EDP SYSTEMS

7.1 Comparison to Manual Systems

As the second standard of field work indicates, the auditor obtains an understanding of the internal control structure to plan the audit and determine the nature, timing, and extent of tests to be performed. The means to accomplish this objective depends upon whether the entity's system is a manual or an EDP system.

EDP systems have similarities and differences from manual systems in the control environment, accounting system, and control procedures.

7.2 Control Environment

A control environment conducive to internal control measures is desirable for both a manual and EDP system. Environmental factors relate to management methods, organizational and budgetary plans and internal verification.

In an EDP system, management must be alert to changing technology, delegation of authority to the EDP department, proper security for EDP, and be willing to make a commitment to install up-to-date hardware, software, and sophisticated control procedures.

7.3   Accounting System

An accounting system for both a manual and EDP system should permit a consistent, easy-to-follow recording of all transactions, that is, with proper documentation, a chart of accounts, and a manual of accounting policies.

The accounting system for EDP processing contains the same elements as a manual system, but allows for a more detailed chart of accounts and simultaneous and automatic processing of transactions in several records, for example, subsidiary and control accounts. Processing of each transaction in a manual system takes place chronologically. In contrast, an EDP system uses two methods of processing transactions—batch processing and on-line processing.

7.3.1 Batch and On-line Processing

Batch processing involves collecting and processing a series of transactions in one lot. On-line processing pertains to the use of peripheral devices that process each transaction as it occurs and transmit the data to the central processing unit of the computer.

7.4   Control Procedures

Control procedures designed to achieve segregation of duties are vital to efficient operation of an internal control system. Despite the integration of several functions in an EDP system, segregation of duties continues to be an important element of internal control just as it is in a manual system. In most cases, an incompatible integration of duties will cause no problems because a suitable computer program will not be manipulative; in a few instances where the EDP department has combined incompatible duties, so-called compensatory controls, are necessary to prevent computer intervention.

The EDP department should have segregation of duties in programming, computer operation, and file maintenance. Combination or integration of two or more of these duties requires such compensating controls as restricted access to EDP programs, equipment and data files. These compensating controls may fall into one or both categories of control procedures: general controls and application controls.

7.4.1 General Controls

General controls relate to all EDP applications and include organization and operation controls, systems development and documentation controls, hardware and systems software controls, access controls, data and procedural controls. Both manual and EDP systems depend on general controls but, in the case of EDP systems, the emphasis depends more on the integrity of the computer system rather than trustworthy personnel.

Segregation of functions in an EDP system concerns the organization of an EDP department where programming, separation of computer operation, and file maintenance is essential. In a manual system, separate persons or departments handle authorization, recording, execution, and custody of assets. Except for authorization, an EDP system combines these functions.

Systems development and documentation controls in an EDP system consist of procedures designed to ensure the integrity of computer storage devices and systems documentation. Such controls consist of magnetized internal or external labels to prevent processing of incorrect files, back-up filing, or filing of duplicate programs and data to insure availability of records. Computer documentation also consists of program listings, error listings, logs, and manuals. A manual system would not need any comparable controls, except for serially-numbered documents and copies of data.

Hardware and systems software controls are unique to EDP systems and nothing comparable applies to manual systems. An example of such controls is the parity check, an internal computer check against malfunction in the machine's movement of data.

Access controls are operating procedures designed to prevent unauthorized modifications to data files and programs or misuse of computer hardware. These controls, such as passwords and logs, assist in preventing or detecting errors or irregularities caused by misuse or manipulation of data files, or unauthorized or incorrect use of a computer program. A manual system would have similar precautions—use of security devices, such as cash registers, sales registers, safes and vaults, locked storerooms, and sign-in procedures for access to files or data.

Data and procedural controls provide a framework for control of daily operations and protection against processing errors. Examples of such controls are a written manual of systems and procedures for all computer operations, internal verification of systems and computer processing activities. Similar controls exist in a manual system where the accounting system includes a manual of accounting policies and procedures with internal audits or verification acting as a system of checks and balances.

7.4.2 Application Controls

Application controls are internal controls related to specific accounting tasks—the recording, processing, and reporting of such processing applications as credit sales and cash receipts. Such controls are effective only if the general controls are in place and functioning as planned. Specific to accounting tasks, application controls are of three types: input controls, processing controls, and output controls.

Input controls provide reasonable assurance that data received for processing by computers has been properly authorized, converted into machine sensible form and identified, and has not been lost, suppressed, added, duplicated, or otherwise improperly changed. Control over input begins with proper authorization for initiation of the transactions to be processed. When an on-line system is in use, identification numbers of authorized users signal such authorization. In a batch system, another control device is the use of serially-numbered documents to determine the completeness of the data in a given batch. A self-checking number (check digit) when added to an identifying number serves to verify the accuracy of the numeric data during the input process.

Processing controls assure the reliability and accuracy of data processing by testing predetermined conditions and identifying certain types of errors in the input records. Many input controls can also be looked upon as appropriate processing controls. Program controls which are

51

part of processing controls include program controls, comparing a predetermined total to detect missing amounts, duplication, and transposition errors, namely:

1. Item or record count. A count of the number of items or transactions to be processed in a given batch.

2. Control or financial total. The processed total of a series of similar financial amounts, such as the total dollar amount of accounts payable.

3. Hash total. The processed total of a meaningless series of numbers.

Other program controls include:

4. Limit test. A test of the reasonableness of a field of data, given a predetermined upper and/or lower limit.

5. Validity test. A comparison of employee, vendor, and other codes against a master file for authenticity.

6. Self-checking number. A number containing redundant information such as the sum of digits in another number, permitting a check for accuracy on the input of the number or after its transmission from one device to another.

7. Completeness test. A test to ascertain that all information fields are complete.

8. Sequence test. A test to ascertain that data being processed are in the correct sequence.

Output controls assure the accuracy of the processing result and the receipt of the output by only authorized personnel. The EDP control group has the responsibility for distribution of the computer output to authorized recipients and for follow-up of exceptions and errors.

7.5 Understanding the Internal Control Structure

As was the case for a manual system, the auditors, in planning the audit, must obtain an understanding of the control environment, accounting system, and control procedures. The auditors follow the same steps, in acquiring an understanding of the internal control structure of an EDP system, except that these steps focus on controls unique to EDP, as follows:

1. Review of general controls through a review of prior years' audits, inquiries of client personnel, inspection of documents and records, including organization charts and job descriptions, and observations of the company's operations.

2. Documentation of the understanding of the internal control structure through questionnaires or flow charts. The flow charts may include system flow charts which show a series of procedures and flow of documents in sequence and/or program flow charts which show the major steps and logic of a computer program.

7.5.1 Initial Assessment of Control Risk

Based on the understanding they have acquired of the internal control structure through the review of general controls and documentation of the system through questionnaires and flow charts, the auditors can now make an initial assessment of the control risk.

If the assessment finds control risk at the maximum level, the auditor will not do any further testing; if it is below the maximum, then the auditor will perform additional test of controls to support this conclusion.

7.5.2 Additional Tests of Controls

Additional tests of controls similar to those for a manual system will allow the final assessment of control risk. These tests consist of:

1. Observation and inspection of the general controls by walk-through tests, review of authorizations and approvals.

2. Review of application controls. For a batch system the auditor tests the input controls by examination of serially-numbered documents and verifying the computation of batch control totals.

In testing processing controls, the auditors review the procedures conducted by the EDP control group, examine error reports and activity logs. Error reports list the violations of program controls that occurred during the computer processing.

Special techniques for testing program controls include auditing around the computer and auditing through the computer. In the former, the auditor tests both input and output control procedures without utilizing the computer, whereas in the latter the auditor utilizes the computer in testing both the input and processing of data through the application of computer-assisted audit techniques, such as test data and controlled audit software.

A test deck or test data uses fictitious records and transactions to evaluate the adequacy of a computer program or system. To conduct the test, the auditor:

1. Identifies the control to be tested.

2. Obtains or creates fictitious transactions, including records with errors.

3. Processes the fictitious transactions.

4. Compares the processed with predetermined results. If the results are the same, the auditor concludes that the clients' program is operating as planned.

A variation of the test data approach is the integrated test facility. An integrated test facility is the processing of fictitious records and transactions simultaneously with actual data. Comparison of the processed result of the test and actual data verifies whether or not the clients' program is operating as planned.

A controlled program uses a duplicate program under control of the auditor and processes actual data. The auditor can then compare the processed results of the controlled program with the clients' program. If the processing of the actual data through each program takes place simultaneously, the technique is called *parallel simulation*. This technique is especially adaptable to on-line processing where the actual transaction is taking place and being processed at the same time. In this case, the data is so-called live data.

7.5.3 Final Assessment of Control Risk

The guidelines for assessing control risk are the same whether the system uses EDP or manual processing. The assessment determines the nature, timing, and extent of the substantive testing or the evidence necessary for expression of an opinion on the financial statements. In assessing EDP control, the auditor should consider whether certain controls are in effect.

For a batch system, programming and operation should be separate, an independent group should test all programs on a periodic basis, and program controls should include use of batch totals. With an on-line system, users should enter data but other functions should be separate, internal auditors should test all programs and program controls should include record counts. For both a batch and on-line system, the system should use program listing and logs, and provide control totals with input, and users should have access to the master files.

CHAPTER 8

EVIDENCE GATHERING

8.1 Objectives of Gathering Evidence

The objectives of gathering evidence are:

1. To provide a reasonable basis for an expression of opinion on the financial statements.

2. To restrict audit risk, that is, to give the auditors reasonable assurance about the reliability of information regarding the financial statements.

8.2 Competence of Evidence

The competence of evidence refers to its quality or reliability. Evidence is competent, if it is valid and relevant. Certain conditions lead to competence of evidence, namely:

1. Independence and qualifications of the provider. Evidence from independent sources outside the company increases its reliability. Also, evidence obtained from banks or attorneys or other knowledgeable sources is reliable.

2. Quality of the client's internal control structure. The more effective the design and operation of the entity's

internal control structure, the higher the reliability of the obtained evidence.

3. Direct acquisition of knowledge by the auditor. Evidence the auditor acquires by firsthand observation, correspondence, or computation is reliable because such acquisition involves no possible interference from the client or other party.

8.3 Sufficiency of Evidence

Sufficiency refers to the quantity of evidence that the auditor believes is adequate to use as a reasonable basis for forming an opinion. Certain factors contribute to the sufficiency of evidence, namely:

1. Competence of evidence. The quantity of evidence varies inversely with its competence. As competence increases, the quantity of evidence required decreases and vice versa.

2. Materiality of statement items. The quantity of evidence varies directly with its materiality. The more material a financial statement amount, the greater the evidence required.

3. Relative risk of the engagement. The quantity of evidence varies directly with the relative risk. As the relative risk increases (decreases), the quantity of evidence required increases (decreases).

4. Cost of evidence. The auditors must consider the cost of further evidence versus the additional benefit. However, the expense involved in testing does not justify omitting a procedure considered essential to comply with generally accepted auditing standards.

8.4 Relationship of Evidence to Audit Risk

Audit risk is the risk that the auditors may render an unqualified opinion on financial statements that are materially misstated. Components of audit risk are inherent risk, control risk, and detection risk.

Inherent risk is built-in risk which is concerned with the probability of a material misstatement of a financial statement assertion, given no related internal control structure policies or procedures. Control risk is the risk of a material misstatement not being detected by the internal control system. The study and evaluation of internal control, including tests of controls, will determine the extent of control risk.

Detection risk is the risk that the auditor will accept the financial statements as being fair, when, in fact, they are misleading. Detection risk is the only risk that is a function of the competence of evidence. The auditor gathers evidence, including substantive tests to restrict detection risk.

8.5   Types of Evidence

Types of evidence include documentary evidence, observation, inspection, computations, analytical procedures, inquiries, and letters of representation.

8.5.1 Documentary Evidence

Documentary evidence, the most common type, consists of documents that contain details of transactions. The documents are:

1. Generated and held by the client. Examples of this type of evidence consist of client's books and records (general ledger, general journal, special journals, sales invoices, disbursement checks, purchase orders, minutes of meetings). This type of evidence is reliable under a strong internal control system, but otherwise, since it is client-prepared, it may not be objective.

2. Received from outside parties and held by the client. Examples of this type of evidence include vendors' invoices, bank statements, titles to properties, insurance policies, receipts for paid bills. Preparation by outside parties lends reliability to this type of evidence, but client custody makes it less reliable.

3. Obtained directly by the auditors by independent means. Examples of this type of evidence include computations,

analytical procedures, observation of inventory, or inspection of documents. This type of evidence is very reliable since the auditor obtains it directly and it is not subject to bias or alteration.

4. Received directly by the auditor from outside parties. Examples of this type of evidence consist of confirmations or letters from customers, creditors, insurance companies, lawyers and others, including specialists. This type of evidence is very reliable, because the auditors obtain this evidence from independent parties and control its use.

8.5.2 Observation

Observation occurs when the auditors watch the performance of some function, i.e., actual observation of the taking of physical inventory or equipment or the counting of cash on hand. Physical observation of a function pertaining to an asset is very reliable evidence as to existence, but may not be conclusive as to valuation. For example, inventory or equipment may be obsolete or checks counted as cash may be worthless.

8.5.3 Inspection

Inspection is close scrutiny of documents or physical assets on hand. Whereas observation involves watching an activity, inspection means a more intensive visual process. The inspection of supporting documents of title to establish ownership or a contract to determine its terms are effective, if the documents are genuine.

8.5.4 Computations

Computations involve independent calculations by the auditors to prove the arithmetical accuracy of the client's records. Examples of computations include footing and cross-footing columns of figures, calculating earnings per share, depreciation expense, allowance for doubtful accounts, provisions for federal and state income taxes.

8.5.5 Analytical Procedures

Analytical procedures involve the study and comparison of the appropriate relationships among both financial and nonfinancial data to identify unusual differences. Typical comparisons include current financial data to that of prior periods, to industry averages, to budgeted performance and to nonfinancial data. Examples of analytical procedures include comparisons of ratios, such as profit margins, receivables and inventory turnovers, return on investments, as well as comparisons of absolute amounts of revenues, various expenses and certain assets or liabilities. Generally accepted auditing standards require the application of analytical procedures in both the planning and overall review stages of all audits.

8.5.6 Inquiries

Inquiries of the client assist the auditor in understanding the client's business, risk areas, and problems, such as unusual transactions or the collectibility of past-due accounts. Such oral evidence is insufficient in itself, but is useful in identifying situations and corroborating other evidence.

8.5.7 Letters of Representation

A letter of representation is a written statement summarizing certain assertions of management on the validity of the assets and the inclusion of all liabilities of the client. This statement, in one or more letters, says, in effect, that the auditor has had access to all the pertinent information regarding the financial statements. This type of evidence is of very questionable competence and is not a substitute for other more reliable evidence. The letter, which should be signed by both the Chief Executive Officer and the Chief Financial Officer, mainly serves as a reminder that management is primarily responsible for the financial statements.

8.6   Subsequent Events

Subsequent events refer to material events or transactions that occur after the date of the balance sheet but before the completion of the audit and issuance of the audit report. For accounting purposes, subsequent events do not include matters which may affect the financial position or operations of a company, but are not accounting or financial in nature (e.g., work stoppage or strike). Subsequent events relevant to the financial statements fall into two categories:

1. Conditions in existence on or before the balance sheet date and
2. Facts coming into existence after the balance sheet date

8.6.1 Conditions in Existence at Balance Sheet Date (Type 1)

For subsequent events that provide additional evidence with respect to conditions that existed at the balance sheet date and affect the estimates inherent in the process of preparing financial statements, the financial statements should be adjusted for any change in estimates resulting from the use of such evidence. Examples are loss on uncollectible trade receivables as a result of bankruptcy, settlement of litigation for an amount different from the recorded liability.

8.6.2 Conditions Not in Existence at Balance Sheet Date (Type 2)

For subsequent events that provide evidence with respect to conditions that did not exist at the balance sheet date, but arose after that date, footnote disclosure should be provided to keep the financial statements from being misleading. Some examples of transactions which require footnote disclosure even though they occurred after the balance sheet date are sale of a bond or stock issue, purchase of a business, settlement of litigation, loss of plant or inventories as a result of a fire or flood, and loss on receivables resulting from a customer's casualty.

Sometimes, a subsequent event which relates to conditions not in existence at the balance sheet date, but is a new occurrence, may be so material that the usual footnote disclosure is inadequate. In this situation, the auditor elects to present pro-forma statements.

Pro-forma statements present the amounts that would have been reported if the subsequent event had occurred by the balance sheet date. The presentation is generally in a column next to the audited financial statements in order to highlight the effect on the asset or capital structure of the business. An example of such a subsequent event would be a business combination.

8.7   Review for Subsequent Events

Auditors undertake certain procedures which are likely to discover subsequent events, if they have occurred. These include:

1. Examination of the latest interim financial statements and minutes of meetings of the board of directors and stockholders.

2. Scanning of transactions in the month following year-end.

3. Inquiries of management as to loss contingencies, changes in capital stock, debt, or working capital.

4. Confirmation through a lawyer's letter of any pending litigation, unasserted drains, or other loss contingencies.

8.8   Subsequent Discovery of Facts

Subsequent discovery of facts does not refer to subsequent events, but means discovering of facts after the report date. If auditors become aware of facts that would make previously issued financial statements misleading, they should:

1. Advise the client to make appropriate disclosure of the facts to actual or likely users of the financial statements.

2. If the client fails to make appropriate disclosure, inform the client's board of directors of such failure.

3. Notify regulatory agencies with jurisdiction over the client and actual or likely users of the financial statements.

8.9 Subsequent Discovery of Omitted Audit Procedures

Subsequent discovery of omitted audit procedures refers to the auditor's oversight in conducting the audit, that is, the failure to gather sufficient, competent evidence. The auditor discovers the oversight after the issuance of the audit report (which may be in error) and, therefore, should attempt to perform the omitted audit procedures. If the auditors cannot perform the omitted procedures, they should consult their attorney to determine the extent of required disclosures and suitable action.

8.10 Evidence on Related Party Transactions

Related parties refers to the client entity and any other party where one party or the other gets favored treatment by virtue of certain relationships, for example, officers, directors, principal stockholders, family members, or affiliates such as subsidiaries. The relationships increase the possibility of collusion to promote joint interests.

The objective of the auditor is adequate disclosure of related party transactions, since these transactions are not arms-length and may promote the joint interests of the related parties to the detriment of others.

Procedures to detect related party transactions include:

1. Review known sources of related parties—SEC filings, stockholders lists, minutes of board meetings.

2. Evaluate the client's procedures for identifying and properly accounting for related party transactions.

3. Inquire of management about related parties and their transactions.

CHAPTER 9

AUDIT TECHNIQUES

9.1 Audit Working Papers

The audit working papers are the manifestation of the evidence gathered by the auditor and are the connecting link between the client's records and the auditor's report. All the information relevant to expressing an opinion on the fairness of the client's financial statements should be part of the working papers.

9.1.1 Purposes of Working Papers

Audit working papers serve several important purposes, namely:

1. Assist in planning the next audit. Prior year's working papers show the results of the preceding audit, the conclusion on internal control, a time budget, and any special problems encountered. Inexperienced auditors often learn the mechanics of auditing from the prior year's working papers.

2. Provide a record of the audit work, which supervisors and partners are required to review. The audit working papers are the substance for the review of the audit work which is required by generally accepted auditing standards.

3. Serve as a record of the evidence accumulated. The content of the audit working papers indicates the adequacy

of the auditor's examination and the fairness of the financial statements. If required, the auditors can show to regulatory agencies and courts that they followed generally accepted auditing standards.

4. Support the audit report. The auditor's opinion is a direct result of the evidence accumulated and presented in the audit working papers. In addition, the audit working papers contain information useful in ascertaining the fair presentation of the financial statements.

9.1.2 Confidentiality and Ownership of Working Papers

According to Rule 301 of the Code of Professional Ethics, CPAs must not disclose any confidential information obtained in the course of a professional engagement except with the consent of the client. This rule makes audit working papers confidential, since they contain important, but what should be private, knowledge of about the client's business.

Although the audit working papers are confidential, they are the property of the auditor, not the client. The client does not have the right to demand access to them, but auditors will usually provide any information requested. Since the audit working papers belong to the auditor, they generally pass on to the next auditor on the sale of a practice.

9.1.3 Types of Audit Working Papers

The audit working papers consist of the permanent or year-to-year file and the current file of the year under audit.

9.1.4 Permanent File

The permanent file is a collection of audit working papers containing relatively unchanging data that is of continuing interest from year to year, such as extracts of articles of incorporation and by-laws, copies of minutes of directors', stockholders' and committee meetings, study and evaluation of internal control, analyses of such ledger accounts as land and retained earnings, results of analytical review procedures of prior years.

9.1.5 Current File

The current file includes all audit working papers applicable to the year under audit. The types of audit working papers included in the current file are:

1. Audit administrative working papers, including the audit program.
2. Working trial balance.
3. Lead and detail schedules or grouping sheets.
4. Adjusting or reclassifying journal entries.
5. Supporting schedules including analyses, reconciliations, and computational working papers.
6. Original or copies of source documents.

Administrative working papers consist of audit plans and programs, internal control questionnaires and flow charts, engagement letters, and time budgets. The audit program comprises a separate file to improve the coordination and integration of all parts of the audit. The auditors initial each working paper as the audit progresses.

The working trial balance is a working paper that lists the balances of accounts in the general ledger for the current and previous year and also provides columns for the auditor's adjustments (and reclassifications) and the final adjusted balances.

In most audits, the client provides the auditors with a working trial balance after posting of all regular end-of-period entries. The auditor makes adjusting or reclassifying entries as appropriate after examination of each line item in the working trial balance.

Lead schedules or grouping sheets summarize similar general ledger accounts appearing in the working trial balance as single amounts. Each specific account on the lead schedule has details or supporting schedules which show the related auditing procedures performed and conclusions reached.

When the auditors discover material errors in the accounting records, they propose adjusting or reclassifying journal entries. The client must approve all adjusting entries because management has the primary responsibility for the fair presentation of the statements. Reclassifications do not need approval by the client since they do not affect net income or the total amounts of the elements of the balance sheet or income statement.

Supporting schedules are detailed schedules in support of specific accounts in the financial statements. The major types of supporting schedules are:

1. Analysis. An analysis shows the debit or credit activity in an account, transactions which increase or decrease the balance in the account and account for the net change from the beginning to the end of a period. Examples where analysis is suitable include accounts such as marketable securities, notes receivable, property, long-term debt, and equity accounts.

2. Reconciliation. A reconciliation shows the agreement between two independent sets of records. Examples include the reconciliation of bank balances with bank statements, subsidiary ledgers with control accounts, and accounts payable balances with vendor's statements.

The auditor frequently obtains both internal and external documents or corroborating evidence which becomes part of the current file. Examples of such evidence are confirmation replies, copies of client agreements, copies of minutes of directors' and stockholders' meetings, and letters from the client's attorney.

9.1.6 Organization of Working Papers

Well-organized working papers improve the efficiency of an audit and the effectiveness of the review process. The organization of the working papers in keeping with the financial statements is a logical approach. Starting with the individual financial statement items, the auditor divides the various accounts into components that are separately auditable, e.g., accounts receivable with subaccounts such as trade, officer and employees. A lead schedule shows the components of the account or accounts as summarized in the financial statements.

Use of an indexing or coding system facilitates the organization and review of the working papers. An example is an indexing system which designates each balance sheet account with a letter (such as A for cash,

B for accounts receivable, etc.) and each income statement account with a number (such as 10 for sales, 20 for cost of goods sold, etc.).

9.2 Detailed Knowledge of Client's Business and Operations

Before conferring with the client on audit arrangements and issuing an engagement letter, the auditor must acquire a knowledge of the client's business. At the start of the engagement, the auditor needs to expand on this knowledge and examine general records and accounting records as a framework for design of the audit programs. In acquiring knowledge of the client's business needed for a decision on acceptance of a client and details of the engagement, the auditor has limited access to client information, such as accounting policies, financial statements, and tour of plant and offices. For the more detailed knowledge needed for design of the audit programs, the auditor must have virtually unlimited access to client information, including the general ledger and general journal.

9.2.1 Review of General Records

The auditors examine various nonfinancial and financial records to gain the detailed knowledge needed for design of the audit program. They examine:

1. Articles of incorporation and by-laws or the terms of the partnership contract.

2. Corporate minutes book to obtain information on important authorizations of stockholders or board of directors, such as contractual arrangements and other long-term commitments.

3. Government laws and regulations, particularly those of the Federal Trade Commission, Interstate Commerce Commission, Federal Communications Commission, and Foreign Corrupt Practices Act.

4. Correspondence with lawyers, banks, and regulatory agencies.

5. Financial records, such as income tax returns and financial statements of prior years.

9.2.2 Review of the Accounting Records

To establish the integrity of the general ledger, the auditors test its accuracy by footing some of the individual accounts and tracing ledger entries backward to the journals, and journal entries forward to the ledger.

The objectives of testing the general ledger depends on the direction of testing. Tracing of ledger entries backward to the journals establishes support for the postings and meets the generalized audit objective of validity or existence or occurrence; tracing of journal entries forward to the ledger verifies recording of the transactions and satisfies the generalized audit objective of completeness.

To verify that the various journals contain only properly recorded entries derived from actual transactions, the auditor tests accuracy by footing some of the individual columns, vouching entries backward to original source documents, and examining the general journal entries to ascertain that explanations for these entries are complete and understandable, particularly for unusual transactions.

9.3 Audit Sampling

Audit sampling is the application of an audit procedure to a portion of items within a group of transactions or account balances to draw inferences about the characteristics of 100% of the items (population). This expectation will come about only if the sample selected is representative or, in other words, has the same characteristics as the population. Selection of the sample is subject to sampling risk or the uncertainty of selecting a sample that is representative.

9.3.1 Statistical vs. Nonstatistical Sampling

Sampling plans may be statistical or nonstatistical. Statistical sampling uses mathematical measurement techniques to interpret sample results. With statistical methods, the auditor can calculate sampling risk—that is the probability that the sample selected may not be representative of the population. For example, the auditor can mathematically determine, under certain conditions, the probability of the sample not being representative of the population, e.g., five percent or ten percent.

Nonstatistical sampling substitutes the auditor's judgment for mathematical methods and thus lacks a measure of sampling risk. Both statistical and nonstatistical methods involve selection of samples and evaluating the sample results.

9.3.2 Methods of Sample Selection

The auditor selects the sample using one of two approaches: random and nonrandom. Either approach may be used with nonstatistical sampling, but only random selection is compatible with statistical sampling.

Random Selection. A random sample is one where every item in the population has an equal chance of being in the sample because of the nature of the selection process. Three commonly used methods of random selection are random number tables, random number generators, and systematic sampling.

A random number table is a listing of independent random digits arranged in a table to permit selection of random numbers with multiple digits. The proper use of a random number table involves the following steps:

1. Establishing a numbering system for the population and correspondence between the digits of the table and items in the population.

2. Selecting a random starting point in the table and a route for moving through the table.

For example, if the auditor wants to examine five invoices from a population of invoices which are numbered from 100 to 300, and had the following random numbers 109, 156, 456, 500, 220, 296, 601, and 120, then the auditor would select the invoices numbered 109, 156, 220, 296, and 120.

Computer programs called random number generators can provide a list of random numbers for a given population. Use of computer programs requires establishing correspondence between the population numbers which should be unique and random numbers generated by the computer.

Systematic selection is a technique where the auditor calculates an interval, selects a starting point and then the items for the sample, based on the size of the interval. The size of the interval is generally the result of dividing the population size by the number of items to be selected. This selection technique has the advantage of ease of use and flexibility since it is adaptable to a population of unnumbered documents or transactions. The chief disadvantage of systematic selection is the possibility of drawing a nonrandom or biased sample because the population may not be in random order or sequence.

Nonrandom Selection. A nonrandom sample is one where, because of the nature of the selection process, some items in the population may have a greater or lesser chance than others of being in the sample. Three commonly used methods of nonrandom selection are block sampling, haphazard selection, and judgmental methods.

A block sample is the selection of a group of consecutive transactions or items in a selected numerical or alphabetical order. Selection of a block sample, although convenient, may not lead to a representative sample because a block, no matter how chosen, may happen to be error free (have errors) while the rest of the population may have errors (be error free).

9.3.3 Haphazard Selection

A haphazard sample consists of items selected by the auditor without any particular pattern or any special reason for selecting or omitting any particular items. Haphazard selection may be random, but its unpredictability does not allow the auditor to measure the probability of a representative sample.

A judgmental sample refers to any sample selection process where the auditor makes a conscious decision to include or exclude certain transactions or items from the sample. The auditors may use a judgmental sample when they believe that any other random or nonrandom method of sample selection is inappropriate, e.g., the case of population items with large balances.

9.3.4 Stratification

A technique available for use with any of the random or nonrandom methods of sample selection is stratification. Stratification is dividing a population into groups, called strata, with common characteristics, thereby reducing the variability of the items in each group. The auditor selects a sample from the groups using any acceptable method and evaluates the results separately or combined. Because the overall variability of the population is less, the sample size necessary for evaluation is usually smaller than would be the case without stratification.

9.3.5 Sampling Plans

Nonstatistical sampling endeavors to resolve the same issues as statistical sampling, that is:

1. Strengths and weaknesses of the internal control structure (tests of controls).

2. Fairness of the monetary amounts in the financial statements (substantive tests).

Statistical sampling addresses the objectives of sampling with more formal, organized methods or sampling plans or procedures designed to accomplish the objectives. Sampling plans are of two types:

1. Attributes sampling plans for testing internal control procedures (tests of controls).

2. Variables sampling plans for testing the numerical amounts in account balances (substantive tests).

Whether the sampling plan is an attributes or variables sampling plan, its implementation involves knowledge of the interrelationships among certain statistical concepts, namely:

1. Non-sampling risk.

2. Sampling risk.

3. Allowance for sampling risk (precision).

4. Reliability or confidence level.

Nonsampling risk is the uncertainty which exists even if the auditor examines all of a group of transactions or an entire account balance. This risk arises from incorrect audit procedures (e.g., using only vendor invoices to support accounts payable), misapplication of a correct procedure (e.g., failure to search for unrecorded accounts payable), or misinterpretation of an audit result.

Sampling risk is the uncertainty which is implicit when the auditor examines less than all of a group of transactions or an entire account balance. Proper execution of random sampling methods may control, but cannot eliminate, sampling risk, since it is an inherent part of sampling.

In performing attributes sampling or tests of controls, sampling risk consists of:

1. Underreliance on internal control or the possibility that the sample results will cause the auditors not to rely enough on a control procedure and, therefore, assess control risk at too high a level.

2. Overreliance on internal control or the possibility that the sample results will cause the auditors to rely too much on a control procedure and, therefore, assess control risk at too low a level.

For variables sampling or substantive tests, sampling risk consists of:

1. Incorrect rejection of a population or the possibility that the sample result will indicate a material error in the population which, in fact, does not contain such an error.

2. Incorrect acceptance of a population or the possibility that the sample results will indicate the absence of a material error in the population which, in fact, does contain such an error.

The sample, since it is only a sample, will not usually reflect exactly the characteristics of the population, that is, sampling risk goes with sampling. With statistical sampling, the auditors can specify the sampling risk they are willing to accept by setting, above or below the sample results, a range within which the true results of the population characteristics will probably fall. For example, if a sample indicates an error rate in a control procedure of four percent, the auditor can specify an interval of plus or minus two percent and state the risk of overreliance that the sample result will not exceed a six percent error rate that may be acceptable or tolerable. This range or interval is the allowance for sampling or precision—the closeness or the accuracy—of the sample results to the true population values.

A dollar value interval also measures the allowance for sampling risk or precision applicable for estimating the dollar amounts of groups of transaction or account balances, for example, an interval of $5,000 may be the tolerable range of values that would be acceptable to the auditor for an inventory balance.

The tolerable occurrence rate or tolerable error amount measures the acceptable rate or amount the auditor can justify without either revising the assessment of control risk or the conclusion on the fair presentation of the financial statements.

Attributes Sampling. An attributes sampling plan is one which enables an auditor to evaluate internal control by estimating the rate of deviation from established control procedures in a population. Use of an attributes sampling plan calls for documentary evidence such as the completed form or initials of the person performing the procedure.

The objective of attributes testing depends on the definition of an attribute, a deviation or exception from these attributes and the population to which the attributes and deviations relate. Only established control procedures which provide documentary evidence are attributes. Deviations are errors of commission or omission or control failures relevant to the effectiveness of the control procedures. For example, verifying the accuracy of sales invoices may be a control procedure; failure to verify as shown by not initialing the invoices is a deviation. The auditor must define the population being tested since it may have limits in terms of time or place, e.g., one or more months or geographical location of the entire company.

The sample size in attributes sampling depends on the population size, the tolerable deviation rate, the acceptable risk of overreliance and the estimated population deviation rate. Population size affects sample size directly, but only slightly. The other factors have a much greater effect.

The tolerable deviation rate represents the maximum percentage of control violations which the auditor will accept without reducing the assessed control risk. Establishing the tolerable deviation rate depends on the auditor's judgment and is a question of the significance of the attributes and its materiality in a qualitative sense. Sample size is inversely related to the tolerable deviation rate, i.e., a small tolerable deviation rate means a larger sample size.

Acceptable risk of overreliance on internal control is the risk that the auditor will accept a control procedure as effective when, in fact, it is not and the population deviation rate is higher than the tolerable deviation rate.

If the auditor places too much reliance on the internal control, the assessment of control risk will be at too low a level and will likely lead to a reduction of the nature and extent of the substantive tests. The result will be a higher detection risk and a diminishing of the overall effectiveness of the audit in uncovering material misstatements in the financial statements. Sample size is directly related to the acceptable risk of overreliance, i.e., the degree of reliance increases (decreases) with sample size.

Sample size for attributes sampling also depends on the estimated population deviation rate. An advance estimate of this amount is necessary to arrive at a suitable sample size. The auditor can use the results of the preceding year's audit or a preliminary sample of the current population for this advance estimate.

Variables Sampling. A variables sampling plan is one which enables an auditor to evaluate the fairness of financial statement balances by estimating the audited value of an amount in the total population.

The objective of variables sampling is to determine the proper amount of the sample and thereby provide a fair estimate of a financial statement account. In most variables sampling plans, the characteristic of interest is the projected error, which is the difference between the estimated and recorded amounts.

Ratio Estimation. Ratio estimation uses a sample to estimate the ratio of audited (correct) value of a population to its book value. Multiplying this estimated ratio by the total book value of the population yields an estimate of the correct population value.

Difference Estimation. Difference estimation uses a sample to estimate the average difference between the audited and book value of items in the population. Dividing the net difference between the audited value and book value of a sample by the number of items in the sample yields an estimate of the average difference by the number of items in the population yields the total difference between the book value of the population and its estimated correct value.

9.4   Audit Objectives

The financial statements are the representations of management. As such, the financial statements implicitly or explicitly contain assertions regarding the account balances.

The auditor's objectives are to provide reasonable assurance that management's assertions are valid. These assertions are:

1. Existence or occurrence.
2. Rights and obligations.
3. Completeness.
4. Valuation or allocation.
5. Presentation and disclosure.

9.4.1   Existence or Occurrence

Existence means that the assets, liabilities, and owner's equity accounts in the balance sheet exist; occurrence means that all revenues, expenses, gains, and losses in the income statement occurred during the period. For assets such as cash on hand, marketable securities and inventories, physical inspection verifies existence of the asset. When assets are in the custody of others, such as cash in banks, accounts and notes receivable, direct confirmation with the outside party is the appropriate audit procedure. As for the income statement, testing the occurrence of revenues, expenses, gains, and losses may involve such auditing procedures as vouching, computations, and analytical procedures.

9.4.2   Rights and Obligations

Rights refers to ownership of the assets or rights to use the assets; obligations refers to the debt or liabilities of the entity. For example, the entity may have title which conveys rights to property or may have a lease which also has certain rights regarding the property. When the entity incurs an expense or receives assets for which it does not pay, then it assumes an obligation or debt.

Procedures to verify existence of cash and marketable securities also establish ownership. Physical inspection of plant and equipment verifies existence, but calls for other evidence to establish ownership.

9.4.3 Completeness

Completeness states that the financial statements include all assets, liabilities, equity, revenue and expenses, gains and losses. For example, the accounting records reflect all assets in their entirety and all liabilities which the entity owes. This assertion means the inventory count has left nothing out and the accounts payable balance represents all the obligations to vendors.

9.4.4 Valuation or Allocation

Valuation means that the amounts shown for assets, liabilities, equity, revenues, expenses, gains, and losses are appropriate. For example, the valuation basis for property is historical cost while that for accounts receivable is net realizable value.

Allocation refers to the systematic spreading out of the cost over the accounting periods. This allocation may be depreciation for property or amortization for intangible assets.

9.4.5 Presentation and Disclosure

Presentation and disclosure deals with the proper classification, description, and disclosure of components of the financial statements. For example, presentation of obligations as long-term liabilities in the balance sheet means that they will not mature within one year. Likewise, classification of an item as extraordinary implies that it is unusual in nature and infrequent in occurrence. Overall, the presentation and disclosure is in accordance with generally accepted accounting principles.

CHAPTER 10

REVENUE AND COLLECTION CYCLE

10.1 Functions in the Cycle

The revenue and collection cycle relates to the sale of goods and receiving payment for the goods sold.

10.1.1 Processing Customer Orders

The customer order is the starting point for the entire cycle. The receipt of the customer order results in the writing of the sales order.

10.1.2 Granting Credit

A properly authorized person must approve credit to the customer for sale on account before shipment of goods, in order to prevent sales to poor credit risks.

10.1.3 Shipping Goods

The company ships goods to a customer pursuant to a shipping document, usually a bill of lading.

10.1.4 Billing Customers and Recording Sales

The company uses the sales invoice for billing customers. It must bill all shipments and must not inappropriately bill any customer more than once for the same items. The sales invoice provides the data for updating the sales journal and accounts receivable subsidiary ledger.

10.1.5 Processing and Recording Cash Receipts

This function involves the collection and recording of cash. The company must deposit all cash received intact in the bank at the proper amount on a timely basis. The deposit provides the data for updating the cash receipts journal and the accounts receivable subsidiary ledger.

10.1.6 Processing and Recording Sales Returns and Allowances

The seller frequently accepts the return of the goods or grants an allowance for defective goods and issues a credit memo for such returns and allowances.

10.1.7 Charging Off Uncollectible Accounts Receivable

The seller writes off an account which is no longer collectible. A write-off most often occurs when a customer files bankruptcy or the account enters collection.

10.1.8 Providing for Bad Debts

The company makes an end of period adjustment to record bad debt expense and its effect on the allowance for uncollectible accounts.

10.2 Original Source Documents

Documents which originate with the revenue and collection cycle documents are as follows:

Customer or Sales Order. A written or verbal request for goods and services by a customer.

Sales Order. An internal document prepared by the sales department from the customer order and used for showing the details of the goods ordered, credit approval and authorization for shipment, if required.

Shipping Order. An internal document, prepared by the shipping department, to initiate shipment of the goods, describing the goods and the quantity being shipped. The original goes to the customer and other copies act as a signal to bill the customer. One type of shipping document is a bill of lading which is a written contract between the carrier and seller for the shipment of goods.

Sales or Customer Invoice. An internal document, prepared by the billing department to indicate the kind and quantity of goods sold, the price including freight, insurance, terms and other pertinent data. The original goes to the customer and other copies provide the information for recording the transaction.

Credit Memo. An internal document, prepared by the billing department, to indicate a reduction in the amount due from a customer because of returned goods or an allowance granted.

Remittance Advice. An internal document, prepared by the billing department, to accompany the sales invoice to the customer. The seller returns it with the cash payment. The advice indicates the customer name, the sales invoice number, and the amount of the invoice on receipt of payment.

Customer's Statement. An internal document, prepared by the billing department and sent to each customer, usually monthly, indicating the beginning balance of accounts receivable, the amount and date of each sale, cash payments received, credit memos issued, and the ending balance owed by the customer.

10.3 Accounting Records

Accounting records which are part of the revenue and collection cycle are as follows:

Sales Journal. A journal for recording sales transactions, indicating gross sales by product line. It provides the data for the debits to accounts receivable and sales returns and allowances accounts.

Cash Receipts Journal. A journal for recording cash receipts from collections, cash sales, and all other cash receipts. It provides the data for the debits to the cash and sales discount accounts and the credit to the accounts receivable.

Accounts Receivable Subsidiary Ledger. A file for recording individual sales, cash receipts, and sales returns and allowances for each customer. The total of the customer account balances in the subsidiary ledger equals the total balance of accounts receivable in the general ledger.

Accounts Receivable Schedule. A listing of the amount owed by each customer at a point in time, prepared directly from the accounts receivable subsidiary ledger and equal to the general ledger balance.

10.4 Errors and Corrective Internal Control Measures

The possible errors and irregularities in the revenue and collection cycle are fictitious sales or cash receipts, unrecorded sales or cash receipts, incorrect sales or cash receipts, misapplication of remittances to customer accounts, and improper classification.

Fictitious sales or cash receipts. A number of internal control measures serve to prevent recording of fictitious sales or cash receipts, thereby establishing existence of all recorded amounts. These measures include:

1. Recording of sales from authorized shipping and approved customer orders and sending monthly statements to customers. Support is lacking in the absence of these documents.

2. Segregating of duties between handling cash and record keeping and independent reconciliation of bank accounts. This segregation of duties provides separate, independent verification of the cash receipts and enhances the proper application of such receipts to the appropriate accounts.

Unrecorded sales or cash receipts. Prenumbering and accounting for all sales orders, sale invoices, shipping reports, and shipping orders help in detecting unrecorded sales or cash receipts, thereby insuring complete-

81

ness of the recording for all sales and cash receipts. Other useful measures include segregation of duties between cash handling and record keeping with independent verification of receipts and immediate endorsement of incoming checks.

Incorrect sales and cash receipts. Internal verification of invoices for mathematical accuracy and independent reconciliation of the bank account provides evidence of the recognition of the correct amounts of sales and cash receipts.

Improper classification. Use of an adequate chart of accounts assists in financial statement presentation with proper classification.

Improper classification (presentation and disclosure). Use of an adequate chart of accounts for proper presentation of sales and receivables and also cash balances.

10.5 Tests of Controls

The auditors obtain an understanding of internal control of the revenue and collection cycle, assess control risk, design additional tests of controls and then perform tests of controls related to the audit objectives or management assertions of existence, completeness, valuation and allocation, and presentation and disclosure.

10.6 Substantive Tests for Detection of Misstatements

10.6.1 Audit of Accounts Receivable

The objectives in the audit of accounts receivable are to establish that:

1. Recorded receivables are valid (existence).
2. All receivables are recorded (completeness).
3. Receivable schedules are mathematically correct and agree with the general ledger. Net realizable value is the basis for receivables valuation (valuation).

4. Receivable balances follow appropriate classification by categories with disclosure of pledged and related party receivables (presentation and disclosure).

Obtain an aging schedule of accounts receivable. The auditors obtain an aging schedule of trade accounts receivable at the balance sheet date, foot and cross-foot, test postings, and trace some accounts to the accounts receivable subsidiary ledger.

Confirm receivables with debtors. Confirmation is direct communication with outside third parties who transmit directly to the auditors. This procedure for receivables is the most conclusive step in the verification of accounts receivable. Responses serve to provide the existence of the customer as well as the amount owed and the accuracy of the balance of receivables. The auditors use one of two methods of confirming receivables—the positive and negative methods.

The positive method requests the debtor to confirm directly the balance as correct or not. The negative method requests the debtor to advise only if the balance shown is incorrect. Positive confirmations are best when the receivables balance consists of a relatively small number of receivables with large balances, internal control is strong and the company does not expect the debtors to disagree on the balances shown. Negative confirmations are preferable when the receivables balance consists of a relatively large number of receivables with small balances, internal control is weak, and the company expects the debtors to respond if the balances shown are incorrect.

Perform analytical procedures for accounts receivable and sales. The auditors compute several ratios and relationships to indicate the overall reasonableness of amounts shown for accounts receivable and sales. These computations include the gross profit rate, the accounts receivable turnover, ratio of accounts written off compared to ending balance of accounts receivable, ratio of valuation allowance to accounts receivable. Comparison of the current year with the prior year or industry averages may bring out variations which warrant investigation.

Determine the adequacy of allowance for doubtful accounts. Fair presentation of receivables requires that they be reported at net realizable value, or at face-value less an adequate allowance for uncollectible accounts. The auditors endeavor to estimate the amount of receivables which will be delinquent. In the absence of payment subsequent to the balance sheet date, the auditors evaluate available evidence to arrive at a reasonable write-off of receivables. Such evidence consists of analysis of the aging schedule, investigation of credit ratings, and review with the credit manager of computed ratios.

Evaluate the financial statement presentation and disclosure. The auditor must determine that the financial statement presents receivables in accordance with generally accepted accounting principles. Adequate disclosure means separate disclosure of related party and pledged receivables with disclosure of the nature of the relationships and the assets involved.

10.6.2 Audit of Cash Balance

The objectives in the audit of cash are to establish that:

1. Recorded cash is valid (existent).
2. All cash accounts are recorded (completeness).
3. Cash schedules are mathematically correct and agree with the general ledger (valuation).
4. Presentation and disclosure of cash, including restricted funds, is adequate.

Confirm cash balances with banks. A direct approach to establishing the validity of the cash balance is to send letters to banks that the company has used during the year. The company prepares the confirmation letters but the auditor mails them and receives the replies from the bank. The standard form mailed out by the auditors also requests information on notes owed by the company, contingent liabilities, and security agreements.

Review bank reconciliations prepared by the company. The auditors test the bank reconciliations to verify whether the recorded bank balance is the same amount as the actual cash in the bank except for deposits in transit, outstanding checks, and other reconciling items. Any checks outstanding for a year or more warrant investigation and write-offs may be in order.

Perform a proof of cash. Whereas the bank reconciliation shows agreement of balances at a specific date, the proof of cash reconciles the bank record of cash activity with the accounting records for a period. The proof of cash is a four-column bank reconciliation which bridges two reconciliations and reconciles deposits with cash receipts and checks written with cash disbursements. The auditors compare the amount and date of the cash deposits with the amount and date of cash receipts. Vouching of disbursements to supporting evidence such as vouchers, vendor's invoices, and payroll records and accounting for the sequence of issued check numbers are important steps in reconciling the accounting records with the bank activity.

Obtain a cut-off bank statement for a partial period. The bank reconciliations are more meaningful when the auditors verify the reconciling items. A bank cut-off statement which covers a seven to ten day period after the balance sheet date should show that the year-end reconciliation items have cleared the bank. The return of cancelled checks with the statement may also bring to light checks written before year-end which should have been outstanding on the year-end reconciliation. Thus, the cut-off bank statement provides evidence that the cash balance reflects all checks written before the balance sheet date.

Trace all bank transfers for the week just before and after the audit year. This procedure may disclose overstatements of cash balances resulting from kiting. Kiting involves manipulations causing an amount of cash to be included simultaneously in the balance of two or more bank accounts. A schedule of bank transfers on both sides of the balance sheet date shows the dates of the receipts and disbursements of cash recorded in the cash journals and on the bank statements. Comparison of dates will bring out any manipulation of the cash balance, since the increase in one bank account should be equal to the decrease in another account.

Determine proper financial statement presentation and disclosure. The amount shown for cash should differentiate restricted from unrestricted funds, such as bond sinking fund payments, and compensating balances serving to notify all other funds are for general use. Footnote disclosure may also provide additional information.

CHAPTER 11

ACQUISITION AND PAYMENT CYCLE

11.1 Functions in the Cycle

The acquisition and payment cycle consists of functions reflecting the purchase of inventories and property, plant, and equipment and the payment for these acquisitions.

11.1.1 Processing Purchase Orders

The requisition for materials or property is the starting point for the entire cycle. After approval of the requisition, the acquisition begins with the initiation of an order to purchase the items. A purchase order specifies the item, price, and delivery date. A copy of the purchase order remains with the purchasing department, another goes to the receiving department with quantities omitted, and the third copy provides information to the accounting department.

11.1.2 Receiving Goods

The receipt of the items from the vendor is the point at which recognition of the liability takes place. With receipt of the materials or property, the receiving department initiates a receiving report as evidence of the quantity and condition of the items.

11.1.3 Storing and Issuing Goods

On delivery, the custodian or stores department acknowledges receipt, counts and inspects the materials or property, and notifies the accounting department of actual storage. The stores department issues only those items indicated on an authorized prenumbered requisition. A copy of the requisition remains in the stores department, another goes to the requisitioning department, and the third copy is a notice to the accounting department.

11.2 Original Source Documents

Original source documents used in the acquisitions and payments cycle include:

Requisition. A written request by an authorized employee to the purchasing department to place an order for materials or property.

Purchase Order. An internal document prepared from the requisition and used for showing the details of the items ordered.

Receiving Report. An internal document prepared by the receiving department at the time of the receipt of materials or property describing the items and the quantity and date received.

Purchase or Vendor's Invoice. An external document that gives the amount of money owed to the vendor for a purchase.

Vendor's Statement. An external document sent by each vendor, usually monthly, indicating the beginning balance of accounts receivable, the amount and date of each purchase, with payments remitted and the ending balance owed by the company.

11.3 Accounting Records

Accounting records used in the acquisition and payment cycle include:

Purchases Journal. A journal for recording purchase transactions, indicating the amount of purchases by product line. It provides the data for the credits to accounts payable and purchase returns and allowances.

Cash Disbursements Journal. A journal for recording cash disbursements for credit and cash purchases and all other cash payments. It provides the data for the credits to the cash and purchase discounts account and the debit to the accounts payable at the amount of the original purchase.

Property, Plant, and Equipment Subsidiary Ledger. A file for recording individual requisitions of property with recording of depreciation by year-end total. The total of the individual items equals the total balance in the general ledger.

Accounts Payable Subsidiary Ledger. A file for recording individual purchases, cash disbursements, and purchase returns and allowances for each vendor. The total of the vendor account balances in the subsidiary ledger equals the total balance of accounts payable in the general ledger.

Accounts Payable Schedule. A listing of the amount owed to each vendor at a point in time prepared directly from the accounts payable subsidiary ledger and equal to the general ledger balance.

11.4 Errors and Corrective Internal Control Measures

The possible errors and irregularities in the acquisition and payment cycle are fictitious purchases, unrecorded purchases, incorrect purchases and accounts payable, misapplication of payments to vendor accounts, and improper classification.

Fictitious purchases. A number of internal control measures serve to prevent recording of fictitious purchases, thereby establishing existence of all recorded amounts. These measures include:

1. Use of a vouchers payable system whereby approval of a purchase via a voucher payable requires supporting documents—purchase requisition, purchase order, receiving report, and vendor's invoice.

2. Adherence to a policy of approval of purchases over a certain amount.

3. Internal verification of vendors' invoices, receiving reports, purchase orders, and purchase requisitions.

Unrecorded purchases. Prenumbering and accounting for all purchase orders, receiving reports, and vouchers help in detecting unrecorded purchases, thereby insuring completeness of the recording for all purchases and accounts payable.

Incorrect purchases and accounts payable. Internal verification of calculations and amounts of purchases and disbursements in the accounts payable subsidiary ledger with comparison to the trial balance totals and the general ledger control account provides evidence of the recognition of the correct amounts of purchases and cash payments.

Improper classification. Use of an adequate chart of accounts assists in financial statement presentation with proper classification.

11.5 Tests of Controls

The auditors obtain an understanding of internal control of the acquisition and payment cycle, assess control risk, design additional tests of controls and then perform tests of controls related to the audit objectives or management assertions of existence, completeness, valuation, and presentation and disclosure.

11.6 Substantive Tests for Detection of Misstatements

11.6.1 Audit of Property, Plant, and Equipment

The objective in the audit of property, plant, and equipment is to determine that property, plant and equipment, and depreciation are fairly stated in the financial statements. To achieve this objective, the auditor will establish that:

1. Additions represent actual property installed or constructed (existence).

2. Additions and retirements have all been recorded with removal of costs for retirements and related depreciation from the property accounts.

3. Property accounts reflect additions and retirements as well as accumulated depreciation (valuation).

4. Presentation and disclosure of property, plant, and equipment includes balances by major classes of depreciable assets and the methods of computing depreciation.

Vouch additions to property during the year. The auditors examine vendors' invoices and receiving reports relating to property accounts as well as closely related accounts to verify the recording of an asset for capitalized items and installment basis acquisitions with the unpaid installments set up as liabilities.

Examine rent and lease agreements to ascertain the proper classification of capital leases. If the leases are in fact installment purchases, then they should be accounted for in accordance with the provisions of Statement 13 of the Financial Accounting Standards Board which specifies the criteria of accounting for a capital lease.

Analyze repair and maintenance expense accounts. The auditors review the company's policy for the minimum expenditure to be capitalized and analyze the repair and maintenance expense accounts to determine whether this policy is in effect. Vouching to vendors' invoices and material requisitions provides evidence for distinguishing between capital and revenue expenditures (i.e., asset or expense recognition).

Verify retirements of property. The starting point for verification is the client's schedule of recorded retirements, but the chief objective is to detect unrecorded retirements. Various procedures serve to bring to light unrecorded retirements.

1. Ascertain whether new equipment replaced old equipment.

2. Analyze gains on the disposal of assets and miscellaneous revenue to determine whether cash received arose from the sale of property.

3. Make inquiries of management and production personnel about the possibility of the retirement of assets.

4. Investigate taxes or insurance coverage to ascertain whether any reduction came about from retirement of property assets.

5. Review rental revenue from real or personal property to ascertain whether a decrease in this revenue indicates retirement of part of this property.

Test the reasonableness of the depreciation expense.

1. Review the depreciation policies of the company and appraise the methods in use.
2. Verify the provisions for depreciation by testing for clerical accuracy.

Perform analytical procedures. The analytical procedures include specific trends and ratios used in judging the overall reasonableness of amounts recorded for property, plant, and equipment. The auditors use ratios and trends such as the total cost of plant assets divided by cost of goods sold or annual output in dollars, pounds, or other units, the current year vs. prior year additions or retirements. In addition, the auditors compare the current year vs. the prior year ratio of depreciation in expense to total cost of property and the percentage relationships of accumulated depreciation and related property accounts.

Evaluate financial statement presentation and disclosure. The balance sheet should present balances of major classes of depreciable assets with accumulated depreciation by major class or in total. The disclosure includes the basis of valuation, either cost for operating assets and estimated realizable value for idle property, the depreciation methods used and property pledged as collateral for loans.

11.6.2 Audit of Accounts Payable

The objectives in the audit of accounts payable are to determine that:

1. Accounts payable in the accounts payable schedules are valid (existence).
2. Existing accounts payable are in the accounts payable schedules (completeness).
3. Accounts payable schedules are mathematically correct, agree with general ledger accounts, and reflect proper valuation (valuation). Transactions affecting accounts payable reflect a proper cut-off.

4. Accounts payable presentation and disclosure is adequate.

Vouch individual amounts in the accounts payable subsidiary ledger to vendors' invoices and statements.

Confirm accounts payable with vendors. This procedure, although not mandatory, may uncover vendors omitted from the accounts payable schedule, omitted transactions, and misstated account balances. Sending confirmations to active, but zero-balance vendors, is a useful method of searching for omitted amounts.

Search for unrecorded accounts payable. Possible sources of unrecorded accounts payable include:

1. Subsequent cash disbursements. Payments made in the subsequent accounting period may represent liabilities at the balance sheet date.
2. Unmatched invoices and unbilled receiving reports. Such unprocessed documents at year-end may involve an unrecorded liability at the balance sheet date.
3. Subsequent vouchers. Inspection of the voucher register may uncover an unrecorded liability at the balance sheet date.

Perform analytical procedures for accounts payable. The auditors compare current year vs. prior year ratios, such as accounts payable to purchases or total current liabilities, cash discounts to total purchases. Significant variations warrant investigation of the reasons.

Evaluate proper balance sheet presentation and disclosure of accounts payable. Proper balance sheet presentation of accounts payable requires separate listing of material amounts payable to related parties. Related parties are directors, principal stockholders, officers, and employees. Secured accounts payable and amounts owing to consignors also require a separate listing. Footnote disclosure may provide additional information.

CHAPTER 12

PAYROLL AND INVENTORY CYCLE

12.1 Functions in the Cycle

The payroll and inventory cycle consists of functions reflecting the application of labor and inventories to the production of goods.

12.1.1 Payroll Phase of Cycle

The payroll phase of the cycle includes a number of functions which are incompatible and should be separate.

A personnel department provides an independent source for interviewing and hiring qualified personnel and also the means to discharge or terminate employees. Segregation of duties in the personnel department restricts access to time cards, payroll records, and personnel records.

Timekeeping consists of counting the hours worked or units produced to determine the gross pay for each employee. An internal control measure over timekeeping is a regular comparison of the time or piecework reports prepared by the timekeeper or supervisors with time clock records or perpetual inventory records.

The payroll department computes the amounts to be paid to employees and prepares all payroll records. The computation of the payroll depends on the work hours reported by the timekeeping department and the pay rates and payroll deductions authorized by the personnel department.

Segregation of the paymaster functions for distribution of the payroll checks serves to prevent theft. The payroll department prepares the payroll checks and forwards them to the treasurer for signature. The paymaster or other employee who has no other payroll duties receives the signed checks and passes them out as each employee submits proof of identity.

12.1.2 Inventory Phase of Cycle

The inventory phase of the cycle includes functions which are part of the acquisition and payment cycle, namely processing purchase orders, receiving goods, storing and issuing goods. In addition, the inventory phase of the cycle includes a number of other functions.

The production department determines the items and quantities of goods to be produced from customer orders, sales forecasts, and desired finished goods inventory levels. A factory superintendent follows the complete production sequence from requisitioned materials to processing and routing to the finished goods storeroom or warehouse.

On proper authorization, normally by a credit approved sales order, the shipping department ships the goods to the customer. A copy of the shipping authorization remains with the shipping department, another goes to the stores department, and the third copy serves as a packing slip with the goods shipped.

12.2 Original Source Documents

The payroll and inventory cycle uses several important original source documents, as follows:

Time Card. An internal document showing name and identification number and the number of hours the employee worked, often prepared automatically by time clocks.

Job Time Ticket. An internal document showing particular jobs on which a factory employee worked during a certain time period.

Payroll Check. A check written to the employee for services performed or time worked, giving the gross pay, deductions, and net pay.

Deduction Authorization Form. A form authorizing payroll deductions, including number of exemptions for withholding income taxes.

12.3 Accounting Records

The production and inventory cycle uses several important accounting records, as follows:

Payroll Journal. A journal for recording payroll checks, indicating gross pay, withholdings, and net pay. The payroll ledger summarizes the data in the journal.

Employee Earnings Record. A file for maintaining total employee wages paid year to date. The record for each employee includes gross pay, deductions, and net pay for each payroll period.

Payroll Ledger. A record of the summaries provided by the payroll journal, showing the gross pay, deductions, and net pay for each payroll period.

W-2 Form. A form, prepared by the payroll department and issued to each employee and the IRS and other taxing authorities, summarizing the earnings record for the calendar year, including gross pay, income taxes withheld, and FICA withheld.

Payroll Tax Returns. Tax forms submitted for predetermined periods to local, state, and federal tax authorities for the payment of withheld taxes and the employers FICA tax or unemployment taxes.

12.4 Errors and Corrective Internal Control Measures

The possible errors and irregularities and corrective internal control measures in the payroll and inventory cycle are fictitious employees or inventories, unrecorded payroll or inventories, incorrect payroll or inventories, and improper classification.

Fictitious employees. Corrective internal control measures to establish existence include:

1. Use of time clocks to record time and approval of time cards by foreman.
2. Segregation of duties between personnel, timekeeping, and payroll disbursements.

Fictitious inventories. A corrective internal control measure to establish existence includes tracing backward—items in the inventory to vendor's invoices to the receiving reports and paid checks.

Unrecorded payroll. Corrective internal control measures to determine completeness include prenumbering and accounting for all payroll checks and independent preparation of bank reconciliations.

Unrecorded inventories. Corrective internal control measures to determine completeness include tracing forward—vendor's invoices to the receiving reports or the paid checks to purchase journal to general ledger.

Inaccurate payroll. Internal verification of calculations and amounts increase the likelihood of an accurate numerical valuation.

Inaccurate inventories. Comparison of quantities and prices in the invoices, purchase orders and receiving reports guard against errors and provide evidence of correct valuation.

Improper classification of payroll or inventories. Use of an adequate chart of accounts and internal verification of classification assist in financial presentation with proper classification.

12.5 Tests of Controls

The auditors obtain an understanding of internal control of the payroll and inventory cycle, assess control risk, design additional tests of controls and then perform tests of controls related to the audit objectives or management assertions of existence, completeness, valuation, and presentation and disclosure.

12.6 Substantive Tests for Detection of Misstatements

12.6.1 Audit of Payroll

The objectives in the audit of payroll are to establish that:

1. Recorded transactions for payroll expense are valid (existence).
2. All payroll transactions are recorded (completeness).
3. Payroll schedules are mathematically correct and agree with the general ledger (valuation).
4. Presentation and disclosure of payroll is adequate.
5. Compliance with government regulations concerning employment has been observed in such matters as social security taxes, unemployment insurance, worker compensation insurance, wages and hours, and income tax withholdings.
6. Compliance with terms of union agreements has been observed in such matters as wage rates, vacation pay, and other items.

Review the payroll journal, general ledger, and payroll earnings records for large or unusual amounts. These large or unusual amounts may be accrued bonuses or commissions or may represent so-called padding of the payroll for fictitious employees or fraudulent wages.

Compare canceled checks with personnel records and payroll journal for name, amount, and date. The auditors should also examine canceled checks for proper endorsement.

Reconcile the disbursements in the payroll journal with the disbursements on the payroll bank statement. Most companies use an imprest payroll account to prevent the payment of unauthorized payroll checks. The company writes a check on its general account to transfer the exact amount of each net payroll to the imprest account just before distribution of the payroll. This transfer simplifies the reconciliation of the payroll bank account.

Recompute hours worked from time cards, gross pay, withholdings by reference to tax tables and forms, net pay. These procedures are the most important means of verifying account balances in the payroll and personnel cycle due to the lack of independent third-party evidence. The auditors also test clerical accuracy by footing the payroll journal and tracing postings to the general ledger and payroll register.

Conduct a surprise observation of a payroll distribution, including control of payroll records and the listing for all employees. The auditors use this procedure to verify that every name on the company payroll represents a bonafide employee on the current payroll list.

Trace compensation of officers to contracts, minutes of director's meetings and other authorization. This procedure verifies the amount to include in the 10K report to the SEC and federal income tax return. The auditors obtain the authorized salary of each officer from the minutes of the board of directors meetings and compare it with the related earnings record.

Test computations of compensation earned under profit sharing plans, commission earnings, and pension payments under authorized pension plans. When bonuses, commissions, or pension payments are significant, failure to record the year-end amounts results in a material misstatement. The auditors verify the recorded accrual by comparing the amount with the amount authorized by the terms of the profit sharing plan or the commission agreement or the pension plan.

12.6.2 Audit of Inventories

The objectives in the audit of inventories are to establish that:

1. Recorded inventories are valid (existence).
2. All inventory is recorded (completeness).
3. Inventory schedules are mathematically correct and agree with the general ledger. Lower of cost or market is the basis for inventory valuation.
4. Presentation and disclosure of inventories includes balances by major classes and the methods of inventory valuation (presentation).

Observe the taking of the physical inventory. The auditor does not take the inventory or supervise its taking, but does assume an active role in the observation. This role includes ascertaining that the recorded inventory is real, actually exists (existence) and that all items includible are part of the inventory (completeness). As part of the observation the auditors endeavor to:

1. Detect any obsolete or damaged goods in the inventory. Such goods are written down to net realizable value. Review of perpetual inventory records may also highlight slow-moving items.

2. Establish a proper cut-off of inventory. The auditors will record the serial number of the final receiving and shipping documents issued before the taking of inventory. A proper cut-off also requires the auditors to examine the purchase invoices, receiving reports and sales invoices, shipping reports for several days before and after the inventory date. In addition, the auditors must be certain that purchases and sales reflect increases and decreases in the inventory in the same accounting period.

3. Verify that the inventory tags are prenumbered and account for all tags. Use of the tags guards against accidental omission of goods from the count and double counting of goods.

4. Make test counts of a cross-section of the inventories. The auditors compare these counts identified by tag margin numbers to quantities posted to the summary sheets used for taking the inventory.

5. Examine the final inventory listing and test extensions and postings to establish clerical accuracy.

6. Make inquiries regarding consignments-in held by the company on its premises and consignments-out held by others. Consignments-out are part of the company's inventories but consignments-in are not. For consignments-in, the auditor reviews contracts and reports from consignors and compares the physical inventory on hand with the records.

Send out confirmation requests to public warehouses and consignees holding inventories. Compare responses with warehouse receipts and consignee reports.

Establish valuation of inventory by evaluating the methods of pricing the inventory. The auditors are responsible for determining that the methods of inventory valuation are in accordance with generally accepted accounting principles. The pricing may follow various flow assumptions, such as specific identification, last-in, first-out (LIFO), first-in, last-out (FILO), weighted average and standard lost, and the valuation on the balance sheet should be at the lower of cost or market.

Verify the actual prices assigned to the inventories. The auditors examine purchase invoices to verify the pricing of raw materials and supplies and trace the pricing of goods, as they move through processing, to test the pricing of goods in process and finished goods.

Perform analytical review procedures. The auditors compare inventories by major categories and also calculate ratios such as gross profit margins and inventory turnover with the prior years. Other ratios and comparisons with budgets or industry statistics provide information on variations.

Evaluate financial statement presentation of inventories. The auditors determine whether any inventories have been pledged and whether the company has entered into any purchase commitments for raw materials or sales commitments for finished goods. Proper disclosure in regard to inventories will include the inventory pricing policies followed by the company and list of the inventories by category, such as raw materials, goods in process, and finished goods.

CHAPTER 13

FINANCING AND REPAYMENT CYCLE

13.1 Functions in the Cycle

The financing and repayment cycle relates to the long-term financing of a business through the issuance of debt (bonds and notes) and equity securities (capital stock) and the repayment of this capital. This cycle also includes the payment of interest and dividends.

13.1.1 Issuing Bonds or Long-Term Notes

The responsibility for issuance of bonds or long-term notes rests with the board of directors. On authorization of the bonds, the company engages an underwriter or sells the bonds on its own. The amount of the issue or loan, the interest rate, the repayment terms, and the assets pledged, if any, are all part of the approved agreement. This agreement or indenture for bonded indebtedness states the terms of the issue and any restrictions on the issuing company, relating to maintenance of working capital, limitation on dividends, and establishment of a sinking fund.

13.1.2 Selling Capital Stock

Besides their responsibility for the issuance of bonds, the board of directors also authorizes the sale of capital stock and specifies the number of shares to be sold and the price per share. An underwriter may sell the issue or the company may sell the stock on its own.

13.1.3 Repayment of Principal and Interest

The accounts payable department automatically issues checks for the payment of interest payable and also the portion of bonds or notes when due. A company may assign the task of these payments, especially bonds, to a trustee and issue a single check for the full amount of the payment to the trustee.

13.1.4 Payment of Dividends

The company may perform the function of dividend payment itself or use the services of an independent dividend-paying agent. If using an independent dividend-paying agent, the company will provide the agent with a certified copy of the dividend declaration and a check for the full amount of the dividend. The trustee then issues checks to the individual stockholders.

13.2 Original Source Document

Documents which originate with the financing and repayment cycle are as follows:

> *Bond or note certificate.* A document which represents a legal obligation and indicates the terms of the instrument, such as interest rates, interest payment dates, and maturity date of the principal.
>
> *Stock certificate.* An internal document which represents entity or legal ownership in an entity. The stockholder has the right to vote and receive dividends, if declared, by the board of directors.

13.3 Accounting Records

Accounting records which are part of the financing and repayment cycle are as follows:

Stock certificate book. A book of serially numbered certificates with attached stubs, each showing the certificate number, number of shares, and name of the stockholder. A new stock certificate replaces a certificate cancelled as a result of a sale or transfer.

Stockholders ledger. A record showing the number of shares owned by each stockholder and used for preparing individual payments and other stockholder contracts.

13.4 Audit Objectives or Management Assertions

The audit objectives or management assertions, in the case of the financing and repayment cycle, are as follows:

1. Recorded interest-bearing debt reflects the actual obligations (existence).

2. Recorded owner's equity reflects the actual ownership interest (existence).

3. All interest-bearing debt is recorded (completeness).

4. All owners' equity transactions are recorded (completeness).

5. Recorded interest-bearing debt reflects accurately the amount of the debt incurred (valuation).

6. Recorded owners' equity reflects accurately the amount of the ownership interest (valuation).

7. Interest-bearing debt and owners' equity are properly recorded according to generally accepted accounting principles (valuation).

8. Interest-bearing debt and owners' equity are properly classified and disclosure is adequate (presentation).

13.5 Substantive Tests for Detection of Misstatements

13.5.1 Audit of Interest-Bearing Debt and Capital Stock

The audit of the financing and repayment cycle does not follow the usual procedures for internal control testing followed by substantive tests. Since transactions are few in number, but large in dollars, the audit program concentrates on substantiating the individual transactions with tests of controls occurring concurrently. Possible misstatements pertaining to debt and equity securities and the auditing procedures to detect such misstatements include the following:

1. Fictitious interest-bearing debt and capital stock (existence).

   a) Confirm notes payable with banks and creditors, bonds with the trustee, and capital stock with the transfer agent and stock register.

      Tracing the information in the confirmation replies to the general ledger establishes the propriety of the amounts recorded as interest-bearing debt and capital stock.

      Where the company maintains control over its own stock issue, review the stock certificate book and the stockholders' ledger and reconcile with the general ledger.

   b) Examine duplicate copies of notes for authorization and corporate minutes for authorization of the issuance of interest-bearing debt and capital stock.

   c) Account for proceeds of all stock issues. Tracing the proceeds to the cash records and bank statements, SEC registration statements and underwriting agreements support the amounts recorded as received from stock issues.

2. Unrecorded interest-bearing debt and capital stock (completeness).

a) Examine notes or bonds paid before, and especially after, the year-end to determine whether they were liabilities in existence at the balance sheet date.

b) Review the bank reconciliation for notes credited directly to the bank account by the bank.

c) Analyze interest expense to uncover a payment to a creditor omitted from the listing of notes payable. Review of interest payments may bring to light any unrecorded interest-bearing debt. Interest expense should equal the interest rate times the principal of the obligation and also take into account amortization of premium or discount.

d) Examine the minutes of the board of directors for authorized but unrecorded notes.

e) Perform analytical procedures. For interest-bearing debt, the relationship between the recorded interest expense and the principal amount of the debt should be in line with the borrowing rate of the company.

3. Inaccurate interest-bearing debt, interest expense, and capital stock (valuation).

a) Foot the list for notes payable and accrued interest and trace totals to the general ledger.

b) Examine duplicate copies of notes and bonds for principal and interest rates and noncurrent or current position.

c) Recalculate accrued interest and amortization of premium or discount.

d) Establish proper cut-off of notes at balance sheet date.

4. Improper presentation and inadequate disclosure of debt and equity securities (presentation and disclosure).

a) Examine balance sheet for proper disclosure of notes payable to banks, trade creditors and related parties, for noncurrent portions, assets pledged as security for notes or bonds, and for restrictions resulting from notes payable or bonds.

b) Review articles of incorporation, by-laws, and minutes for provisions relating to capital stock. This review provides some assurance that capital stock transactions and dividend payments have been in accordance with legal requirements and corporate authorizations.

c) Determine compliance with stock option plans and with other restrictions and preferences pertaining to capital stock. Proper presentation requires disclosure of the number of authorized, but unissued shares, being held in reserve for exercise of stock options.

13.5.2 Audit of Dividends and Retained Earnings

Transactions are few in number so, typically, dividends and retained earnings undergo complete testing—a 100% audit. The procedures are substantive tests but serve a dual purpose since they also serve as tests of controls.

1. *Examine the minutes of the board of directors meeting for the amount of the dividend per share and the dividend date.* This procedure serves to establish the existence or validity of the dividends as well as uncover any unrecorded dividends, particularly if declared shortly before the balance sheet date (existence and completeness).

2. *Review the articles of incorporation relating to the rights and privileges of the capital stock and any indentures on bond issues* to determine any restrictions on payment of dividends (existence and completeness).

3. *Recompute the dividends declared and paid by multiplying the dividend rate by shares outstanding.* Tracing the total amount in this case or, when the client uses a dividend disbursing agent, to cash disbursements verifies the amount paid (completeness).

4. *Test a sample of recorded dividend payments from the payee's name on the canceled check to the dividend records.* This procedure establishes that dividends paid to stockholders are valid (existence).

5. *Ascertain that a liability reflects dividends declared, but not yet paid.* The liability arises on declaration by the board of directors (presentation and disclosure).

6. *Determine the accounting for unclaimed dividend checks.* These unclaimed amounts represent liabilities (presentation and disclosure).

7. *Analyze retained earnings for the entire year, showing every transaction affecting the account.* Tracing the credit (debit) to retained earnings from the income statement verifies the net income (loss) for the year. Examination of the minutes of the board of directors verifies some of the debits to retained earnings, such as for dividends (existence).

8. *Determine whether any transactions that should have been included in the retained earnings balance, but were not.* Possible omissions include capitalization of retained earnings for a small stock dividend or appropriations of retained earnings (completeness).

9. *Examine any agreements or bond indentures to determine the existence of any restrictions in the payment of dividends and disclosure of such restrictions in the footnotes* (presentation).

10. *Examine other debits and credits to retained earnings* and establish their propriety according to generally accepted accounting principles (existence and completeness).

11. *Determine the proper valuation of the prior period adjustments* by examination of documents and records which give detail of the transaction (valuation).

CHAPTER 14

OTHER TYPES OF ENGAGEMENTS AND REPORTS

In addition to audits of financial statements, CPAs deal with other attest engagements and also other assignments with varying levels of assurance.

14.1 Attestation Function

The American Institute of Certified Public Accountants has issued *Statement on Standards for Attestation Engagements* which provides guidance to practitioners in all types of attest services. An attest engagement is one in which a practitioner expresses a conclusion with respect to reliability of a written assertion by another party. The attestation standards establish three types of engagements—examinations, reviews, and agreed-upon procedures.

These engagements involve reports which provide some level of assurance on the information presented in accordance with specified criteria. Examinations which include audits of financial statements provide reasonable assurance. Reviews, which consist of inquiries and analytical review procedures, provide limited assurance conveyed in the form of a negative assurance clause included in the review report in which the CPA indicates the nonexpression of an opinion.

Agreed-upon procedures, which follow procedures requested by the user, provide assurance which varies with the specific procedures agreed to and performed. These reports have limited distribution unlike examinations and reviews which result in general use reports.

14.2 Special Examination Engagements

Auditors work on a number of special examination engagements which result in the issuance of an opinion with reasonable assurance—the highest level of assurance. These special reports cover examinations on:

1. Financial statements prepared in accordance with a comprehensive basis of accounting other than generally accepted accounting principle (e.g., cash basis statements).

2. Specified elements, accounts, or items contained in the financial statements.

3. Debt compliance letters related to audited financial statements.

4. Audited financial information presented in prescribed forms of regulatory agencies.

14.2.1 Reports on Other Comprehensive Bases of Accounting

Departures from generally accepted accounting principles in audited financial statements generally call for a qualified or adverse opinion. Because of this unduly severe requirement, a special reporting format is available for financial statements prepared in accordance with a comprehensive basis of accounting other than generally accepted accounting principles. Use of this format includes accounting using bases derived from cash transactions, income tax law, regulatory agency rules, or price-level reports.

The auditor may issue an audit report which includes:

1. A scope paragraph identifying the statements examined and stating the conduct of the audit in accordance with generally accepted auditing standards.

2. An explanatory paragraph that explains or refers to a note describing the basis of accounting and states that the financial statements do not conform to generally accepted accounting principles.

3. An opinion paragraph that expresses the auditor's opinion on the presentation of the statements in accordance with the basis of accounting described.

14.2.2 Reports on Specified Elements, Accounts, or Items of a Financial Statement

An auditor may render an opinion on specified portions of financial statements. In performing such engagements, the auditor considers materiality in relation to the information presented and generally assumes materiality at a lower level than that in an audit of the complete financial statements.

The auditor may issue an audit report which includes:

1. A scope paragraph identifying the specified elements, accounts, or items examined and stating that the conduct of the examination is in accordance with generally accepted auditing standards and a statement on whether the report is in conjunction with an audit of the financial statements.

2. An explanatory paragraph that explains the specified elements, accounts, or items being examined and the basis for the opinion.

3. An opinion paragraph that expresses the auditor's opinion on the fair presentation of the specified elements, accounts, or items in accordance with the basis described.

14.2.3 Reports on Debt Compliance Letters

Sometimes a client asks an auditor to provide a lender with a report on compliance with specified agreements or regulatory requirements (e.g., restriction on payment of dividends). This report may be a separate report or part of a report that expresses the auditors' opinion on the financial statements by adding a paragraph after the opinion paragraph.

In either event, the auditor should provide a debt compliance letter only for a client pursuant to an audit of the overall financial statements.

14.2.4 Reports in Prescribed Forms

In some cases regulatory bodies and other entities request financial information and auditor's reports on prescribed forms or schedules, such as loan applications or filings with regulatory agencies. The auditor will reword the form or issue a separate report as an attachment to the form.

14.3 Other Reports with Maximum Assurance

In addition to the special examination engagements, CPAs may provide maximum assurance in their reports on audits of:

1. Personal financial statements.
2. Prospective financial statements.
3. Reports on internal accounting control.

14.3.1 Personal Financial Statements

Auditors sometimes render opinions on personal financial statements. These statements follow a prescribed format and show assets at both cost and estimated current values and liabilities at current amounts. The auditors must apply audit procedures that will verify the estimated current values.

An individual's balance sheet or statement of financial condition reflects net worth and includes a liability for income taxes on the difference between the estimated current values of assets and their income tax bases. The income statement or statement of changes in net worth shows revenue and expenses and changes in the estimated current values of assets and liabilities.

If satisfied that the estimated current values present fairly the individual's financial condition and changes in net worth in conformity with generally accepted accounting principles applied consistently, the auditor will issue an unqualified report. When the accounting records are inadequate for auditing purposes, the auditor will issue a qualified opinion or disclaimer of opinion depending on the materiality of this scope limitation.

14.3.2 Prospective Financial Statements

There are two types of prospective financial statements:

1. Financial forecasts. A financial forecast presents information about the entity's expected financial position, results of operations, and cash flows. Financial forecasts may be for general use.

2. Financial projections. A financial projection presents expected results, given one or more hypothetical assumption. The user can then evaluate the effect of the assumption, for example, expansion of the plant, on the financial statements. Financial projections should be for limited use only.

14.3.3 Operational Audits

An operational audit is a comprehensive examination of an operations unit of an organization to evaluate its effectiveness and efficiency. The management advisory services department of many CPA firms perform operational audits for both profit and not-for-profit enterprises. Generally, however, internal auditors or qualified client personnel carry out operational audits.

14.3.4 Reports on Internal Accounting Control

Auditors sometimes render reports on their evaluation of the client's internal control, providing such reports to management, regulatory agencies, other independent auditors, or the general public. The reports may result from an internal control evaluation performed as part of an audit or from a special study on internal control.

A report on internal control differs from a management letter, even if the report comes about from an audit. The management letter is for exclusive use of management, whereas the report on internal control is for general distribution, usually regulatory agencies. For this reason, the letter on internal control calls for the formal precautionary language used in reports to outsiders.

14.4 Reports with Limited Assurance

CPAs frequently do not carry out sufficient procedures for an audit, but may perform limited procedures or a review of the financial statements. This review may be for the annual statements of a nonprofit company or the interim statements of a public company. A review is a form of attestation, using chiefly analytical and inquiry procedures, for the purpose of expressing limited assurance that the financial statements are in accordance with generally accepted accounting principles.

14.4.1 Review of Nonpublic Companies

For performing a review of a nonpublic company, a CPA must make inquiries about the accounting principles and practices of the client's industry, the client's organization, operating characteristics, and the nature of its assets, liabilities, revenues, and expenses. The CPA must also conduct analytical procedures, comparing the actual results of this year with those of last year and the budgets.

14.4.2 Review of Interim Financial Information of a Public Company

CPAs also perform reviews of interim, but not annual, financial information of public companies. The SEC requires disclosures of un-audited quarterly data in a note to the annual financial statements and a review of these data by an independent public accountant.

The procedures applied in a review of interim information consists chiefly of inquiries and analytical procedures. Examples would include inquiries of client management concerning the operation of the accounting system; significant changes in the internal control structure; analytical procedures consisting of comparison of the financial results with prior interim periods and budgeting amounts; reading of minutes and interim financial data; obtaining written representations from management.

14.4.3 Review Report

A review report, whether issued for a nonpublic or public company, consists of three paragraphs. The first is an introductory paragraph, the second describes the scope of a review and explicitly indicates the

113

nonexpression of an opinion, and the third uses a negative assurance clause. A negative assurance clause is an assertion that the CPAs are not aware of any need to materially modify the presentation of the information in order for it to be in conformity with generally accepted accounting principles. Any departure from generally accepted accounting principles should be described in a separate paragraph. CPAs may not issue a review unless they are independent of the entity.

A standard review report should read as follows:

"We have reviewed the accompanying balance sheet of ABC Company as of December 31, 19XX, and the related statements of income, retained earnings, and cash flows for the year then ended, in accordance with standards established by the American Institute of Certified Public Accountants. All information included in these financial statements is the representation of the management of ABC Company.

A review consists principally of inquiries of company personnel and analytical procedures applied to financial data. It is substantially less in scope than an audit in accordance with generally accepted auditing standards, the objective of which is the expression of an opinion regarding the financial statements taken as a whole. Accordingly, we do not express such an opinion.

Based on our review, we are not aware of any material modifications that should be made to the accompanying financial statements in order for them to be in conformity with generally accepted accounting principles."

14.4.4 Letter for Underwriters

Most underwriting agreements require or lead to a request that the auditors issue a letter that they have performed a reasonable investigation of unaudited financial information contained in a registration statement. This so-called comfort letter contains a negative assurance clause or an assertion that nothing came to the auditor's attention which would require modification of the financial statements.

14.5 Reports with Minimum Level of Assurance

Sometimes CPAs provide a minimum level of accounting services or compilation for small nonpublic companies and may also consent to an association with unaudited financial statements of public companies. In those situations involving nonpublic companies, the CPAs perform a so-called compilation. A compilation is an accounting service that involves the preparation of financial statements from the client's accounting records.

14.5.1 Compiled Financial Statements of a Nonpublic Company

Preparing a compilation for nonpublic companies requires the CPA to have knowledge of the accounting principles and practices used within the client's industry and a general understanding of the client's business transactions and accounting records. Beyond reasonable skepticism, the CPAs have no responsibility to perform any investigative procedures to verify the financial information.

A compilation service involves the issuance of a standard compilation report consisting of the following two paragraphs: an introductory paragraph and a second paragraph indicating the nonexpression of an opinion or any form of assurance on the financial statements. A standard compilation report should read as follows:

"We have compiled the accompanying balance sheet of ABC Company as of December 31, 19XX, and the related statements of income, retained earnings, and cash flows for the year then ended, in accordance with standards established by the American Institute of Certified Public Accountants.

A compilation is limited to presenting in the form of financial statements information that is the representation of management. We have not audited or reviewed the accompanying financial statements and, accordingly, do not express an opinion or any other form of assurance on them."

115

CPAs may also compile financial statements that omit substantially all disclosures required by generally accepted accounting principles as long as the report so states in a third paragraph. A separate paragraph may also be useful to discuss any departure from generally accepted accounting principles or give an explanation of compilations of information in forms prescribed by a bank, trade association, or government agency. If the CPAs are not independent of the client, they may still issue a compilation report, although lack of independence precludes an audit or review.

14.5.2 Association with Unaudited Financial Statements of a Public Company

When CPAs become associated with the financial statements of a public company by assisting the company in preparing but not auditing or reviewing those statements, they must disclaim an opinion on the statements. In such situations, the CPAs only responsibility is to read the statements for obvious material errors, mark each page of the statements as unaudited and issue a disclaimer of opinion.